W9-AYE-517

THE ALL-NEW KIDS' STUFF BOOK OF

CREATIVE SCIENCE EXPERIENCES

FOR THE YOUNG CHILD

by Imogene Forte and Joy MacKenzie

Incentive Publications, Inc.
Nashville, Tennessee

Illustrated by Gayle Harvey
Cover by Marta Drayton
Edited by Jennifer J. Streams

ISBN 0-86530-474-2

Copyright ©2001 by Incentive Publications, Inc., Nashville, TN. All rights reserved. No part of this publication may be reproduced, stored in a retrieval system, or transmitted in any form or by any means (electronic, mechanical, photocopying, recording, or otherwise) without written permission from Incentive Publications, Inc., with the exception below.

Pages labeled with the statement **©2001 by Incentive Publications, Inc., Nashville, TN** are intended for reproduction. Permission is hereby granted to the purchaser of one copy of **THE ALL-NEW KIDS' STUFF BOOK OF CREATIVE SCIENCE EXPERIENCES FOR THE YOUNG CHILD** to reproduce these pages in sufficient quantities for meeting the purchaser's own classroom needs only.

PRINTED IN THE UNITED STATES OF AMERICA
www.incentivepublications.com

Table of Contents

How to Use This Book 7

Living Things 9

- Living and Non-Living Things 10
- Living Things in Color 11
- Plant Parts 12
- Missing Parts 13
- How Does Your Garden Grow? 14
- A Flower Garden 15
- A Vegetable Garden 16
- Plants to Eat 17
- New Plants from Old Plants 18
- Plants from Bulbs 19
- Plants from Seeds 20
- Seeds 21
- Fruit, Vegetable, or Flower? 22
- Where Do Animals Come From? 23
- Bird Nests and Eggs 24
- Mammals 25
- Self-Portrait 26
- Farm Animals 27
- Pets 28
- A Special Pet 29
- Zoo Animals 30
- Insects 31
- Animals on the Move 32
- Dot-to-Dot, 1 to 30 33
- Turtles and Snails 34
- Animal Coverings 35
- Dinosaurs 36
- Habitats 37
- Living Things Review 38
- Paste-Up 40

The Human Body 41

- Is Skin Just a Cover-Up? 42
- Temperature Control 43
- Skin Protection 44
- Freckles 45
- Virus 47
- Skeleton 48
- Inside, Outside 49
- Body Parts 50
- Brain Power 51
- How Does Your Heart Beat? 52
- Count Your Pulse 53
- Staying Well and Healthy 54
- Taking Care of Your Body 55
- Good Food for a Good Body 56
- Dinner Time 57
- Exercise Express 58
- Sleepy Time 59
- Do You Know Why People Yawn? 60
- Ahh-choo! 61
- Hot or Cold 62
- Hiccups 63
- How Does a Body Fix Itself? 64
- How Cuts Heal 65
- Living, Growing, and Changing 66

Earth and Sky 67
Exploring 68
Did You Know That the Earth is Round? 69
Water, Water, Water 70
What Makes Day and Night? 71
Night and Day 72
For Use at Night 73
For Use During Daylight Hours 74
My Favorite Season 75
What Makes Summer and Winter? 76
Four Seasons 77
Seasons in Living Color 78
What Do You Know About the Sun? .. 79
Stars 80
Have You Ever Wished Upon a Star? 81
Moon Walk 82
Space Visit 83
Space Ship 84
Do You Know How Sand is Made? 85
Rock-A-Round 86
Rocks of Long Ago 87
Studying Rocks 88

Air and Water 89
Air is Everywhere 90
Experiment with Air 91
. . . More Experiments 92
Living Things Need Clean Air 93
X-Out Litter 94
X-Out Air Pollution 95
Pollution Prevention 96
Color the Rainbow 97
Evaporation 98
Is Dissolving the Same as Disappearing? 99
An Experiment with Water and Ice 100

Machines, Magnets, and Electricity 101
How Do Tools Make Hard Work Easy? 102
Wheels 103
Wheels at Work 104
Farm Tools 105
Tools That Help Care for Plants 106
What Do You Think? 107
For You to Try 108
Which Truck Will Go Faster? 109
An Inclined Plane 110
Take a Big Step 111
Move the Box 112
Many Machines 113
Machines to Make Work Easier 114
Thank Goodness for Machines 115
Can You See Electricity? 116
How Electricity Helps Us 117
Electrical Power 118
Magnets 119

Test Yourself 120

What Have You Learned? 121

Answer Pages . . . Check Yours! 122

This is My World 124

Vocabulary for Science 125

HOW TO USE THIS BOOK

Young children are curious about and extremely sensitive to their environment. They instinctively push and pull; take apart and attempt to put together again; smell, taste, and feel things around them. "Why," "what," "when," "where," and "how" are words they use naturally and often. It is this interaction with the environment that grown-ups can either nurture and encourage or inhibit and retard.

Time to question, explore, wonder, and ponder is basic to the creative nourishment of the scientific attitude in young children. As they discover each new scientific marvel, they should not be pushed to abandon an interest before their natural curiosity has been satisfied. As children are provided with time and help to see relationships and arrive at satisfactory conclusions based on their own observations, explorations, and questioning, the foundation for scientific thinking and action in later life is being built.

At no time in life is it more important for children to understand the world in which they live and their own roles in it. It is at this developmental level that children are building the feelings about themselves that will be with them for the rest of their lives. The security that is to be gained from the understanding of conception, birth, and death as natural and normal, and from acceptance of themselves as biological organisms with bodily needs comparable to all like organisms is reassuring to the young child. This understanding can be broadened to include proper health and safety measures as well as to enhance the development of a satisfying and expanding self-concept.

Exposure to television, radio, and adult conversation enable today's children to accumulate an awesome body of scientific knowledge long before they are ready for school. Often they form false impressions from information gained in this manner.

The purpose of this book is to give children concrete experiences designed to help them sort out and make meaningful use of scattered knowledge and isolated concepts as well as to develop new insights and understandings.

The activities have been structured to encourage an open and creative approach to problem solving and to result in the development of broad major concepts of a scientific nature. They have been planned to correspond to the specific interests of the creative preschool child. Their goal is to encourage children to learn to form generalizations that will be helpful as they expand their horizons and move on to new levels of curiosity and greater interest in understanding themselves and their world. The units may be presented in any order desired so long as the entire unit is treated as a whole and completed in the proper order before another is started. The activities within each unit are developmental in nature and should be completed in the sequence in which they are arranged.

Many opportunities to explore the wonders of nature first hand; to experiment with "real materials"; to gain sensory images in feeling, seeing, touching, tasting, and smelling; and to verbalize these experiences will extend the use of this book immeasurably. As the children are led into paths of divergent thinking, presented with more than one alternative as a possible solution to problems, and internalized the concepts being gained from observation, experimentation, and classification they will develop the desired scientific attitude. More importantly, they will be busy, creatively engaged youngsters capable of enjoying life to the fullest.

Living Things

Living and Non-Living Things

All living things need air, sunlight, and water to grow.

Some living things are plants.

Some living things are animals.

Draw a circle around the pictures of living things.

Color the plants.

Draw and color one more non-living thing.

Name_____

 Copyright ©2001 by Incentive Publications, Inc., Nashville, TN.

Color ten living things.

Draw circles around ten non-living things.

Name_____

 Copyright ©2001 by Incentive Publications, Inc., Nashville, TN.

Plant Parts

Most plants have four parts.

They are roots, stem, leaves, and flowers or fruit.

Color the roots black.

Color the stem brown.

Color the leaves green.

Color the flower yellow.

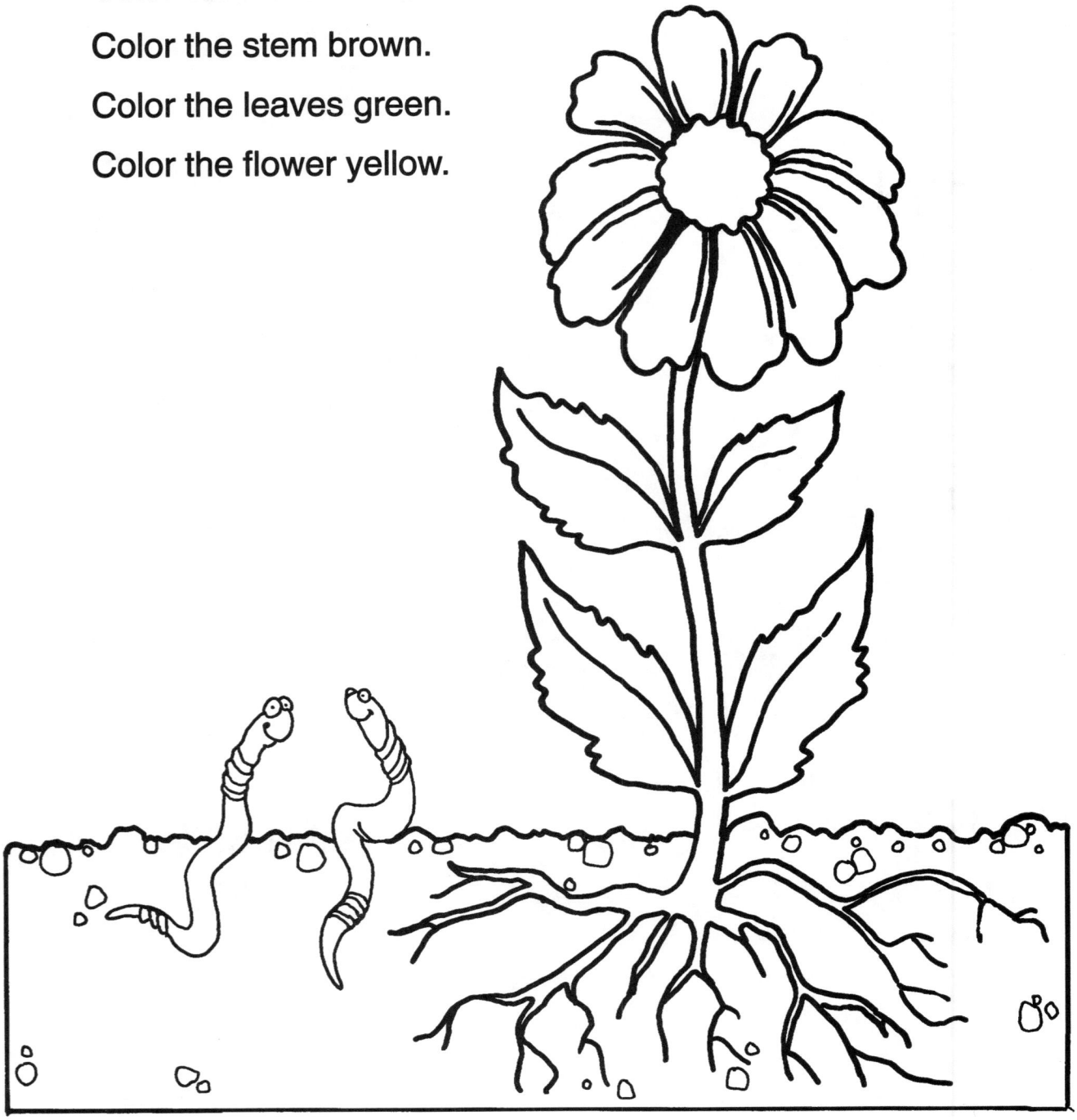

Name_____

 Copyright ©2001 by Incentive Publications, Inc., Nashville, TN.

Missing Parts

Here are some plants with missing parts.

Draw the missing parts.

Name the parts.

Color the plants.

WORD BOX

- roots
- stem
- leaves
- flower

Name_____

 Copyright ©2001 by Incentive Publications, Inc., Nashville, TN.

How Does Your Garden Grow?

Plants need sunlight, water, and air to grow.

The roots of plants grow downward.

The stems grow upward.

Leaves and flowers grow from the stems.

As they grow, they turn toward the sunlight.

Make an X on the vegetables in this garden.
Color the flowers.

Name_____

 Copyright ©2001 by Incentive Publications, Inc., Nashville, TN.

A Flower Garden

Draw a garden filled with your favorite flowers.

Color the flowers.

Write the name of a person you would like to give the flowers to.

Name_____

Copyright ©2001 by Incentive Publications, Inc., Nashville, TN.

A Vegetable Garden

In this garden, draw vegetables you would like to eat.

Say the names of the vegetables.

Draw a circle around your favorite vegetable.

Name_____

 Copyright ©2001 by Incentive Publications, Inc., Nashville, TN.

Plants to Eat

Make an X on the roots we eat.

Color the leaves we eat green.

Draw a circle around the fruits we eat.

Draw a box around the stem we eat.

Name_____

 Copyright ©2001 by Incentive Publications, Inc., Nashville, TN.

New Plants from Old Plants

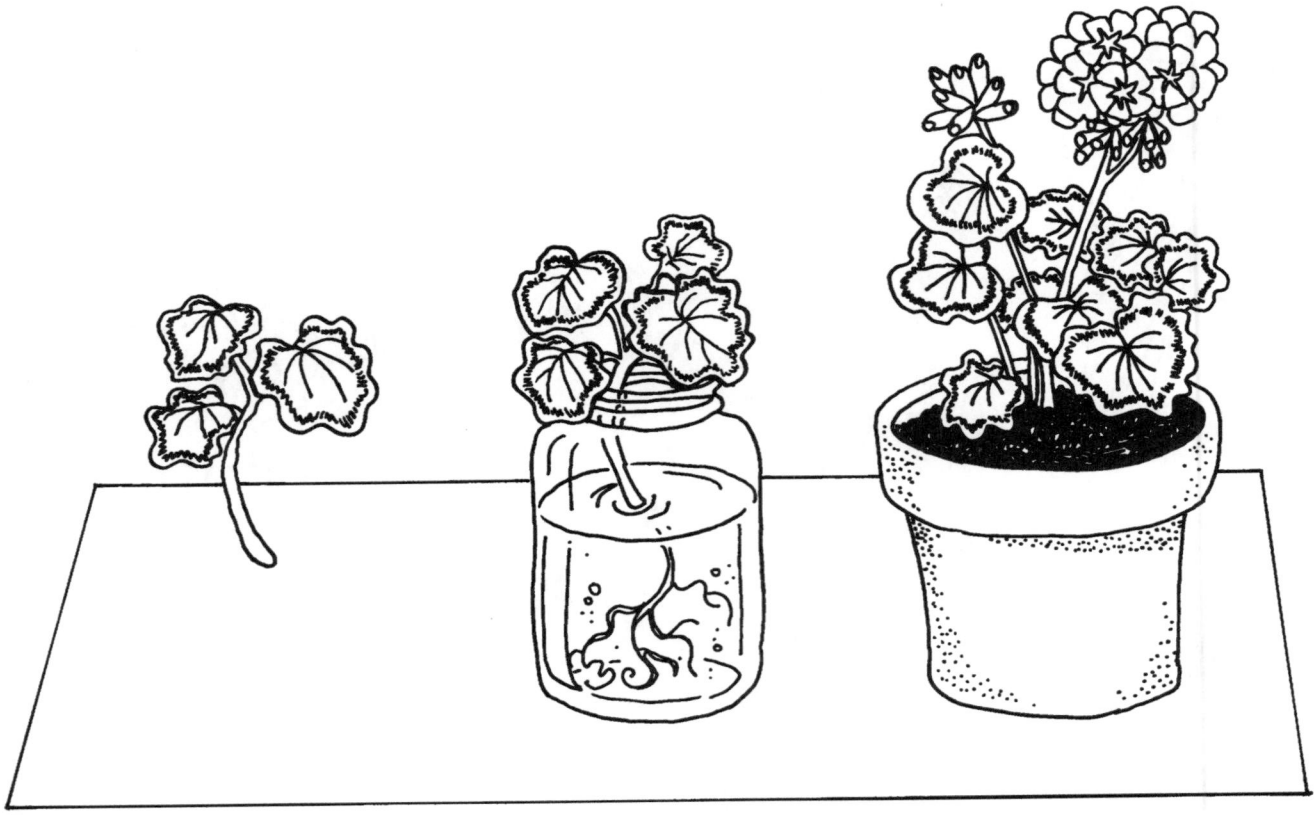

Some plants can be started from cuttings.

A cutting is put in water until it grows roots, and then it is planted in soil.

Geraniums can be grown from a cutting.

Draw a picture of another plant that can be grown from a cutting.

Name_____

 Copyright ©2001 by Incentive Publications, Inc., Nashville, TN.

Plants from Bulbs

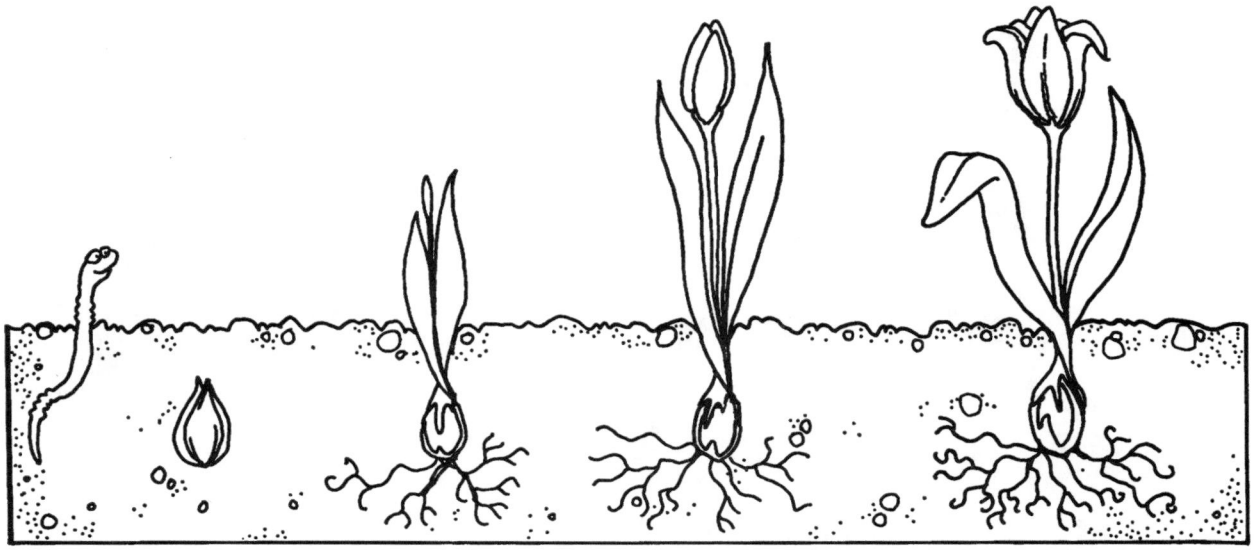

Some plants can be grown from bulbs.

A bulb looks like a ball of roots covered with tiny, dried-up leaves.

It is really an underground bud covered with bud scales.

When you plant the bulb in soil, a new plant comes from it.

Tulips grow from bulbs.

Draw a picture of another plant that grows from a bulb.

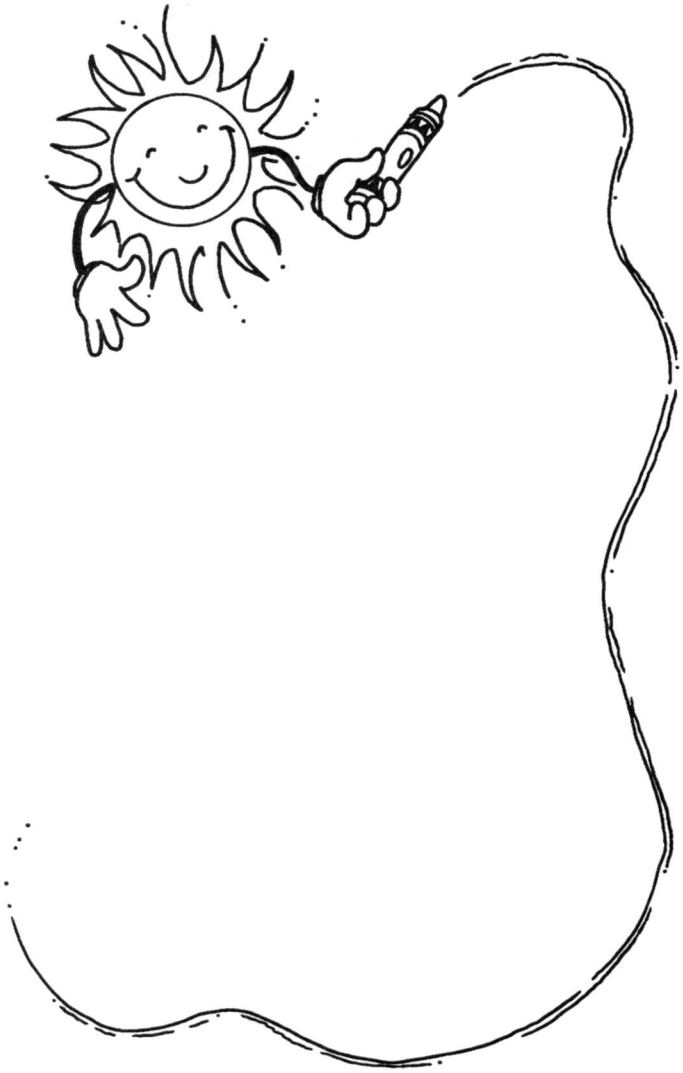

Name_____

 Copyright ©2001 by Incentive Publications, Inc., Nashville, TN.

Plants from Seeds

Many plants grow from seeds.

It seems strange to think of large trees growing from tiny seeds, but they do.

These are pictures of things that grow from seeds.

Draw another plant that grows from seeds.

Have you ever found the magic star in an apple?

If you cut an apple in half, you would see a star with five points.

Count the number of seeds in the star.

There are _____ seeds in the star inside an apple.

Name_____

 Copyright ©2001 by Incentive Publications, Inc., Nashville, TN.

Seeds

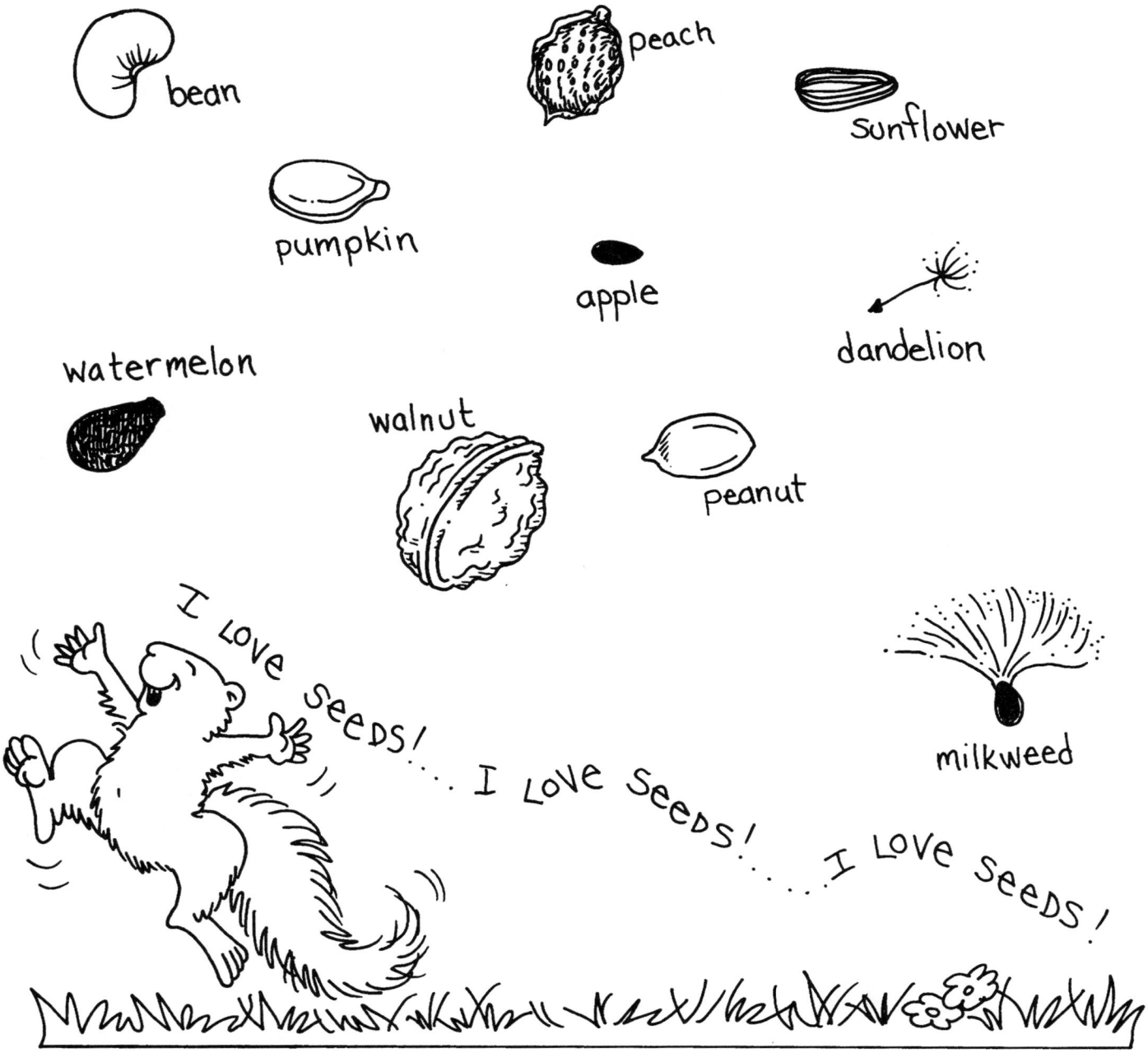

These are seeds.

How many of them have you seen?

Make an X on the largest seed.

Draw a circle around the smallest seed.

Name_____

 Copyright ©2001 by Incentive Publications, Inc., Nashville, TN.

Fruit, Vegetable, or Flower?

Make an X on the picture that is not a fruit.

Make an X on the picture that is not a vegetable.

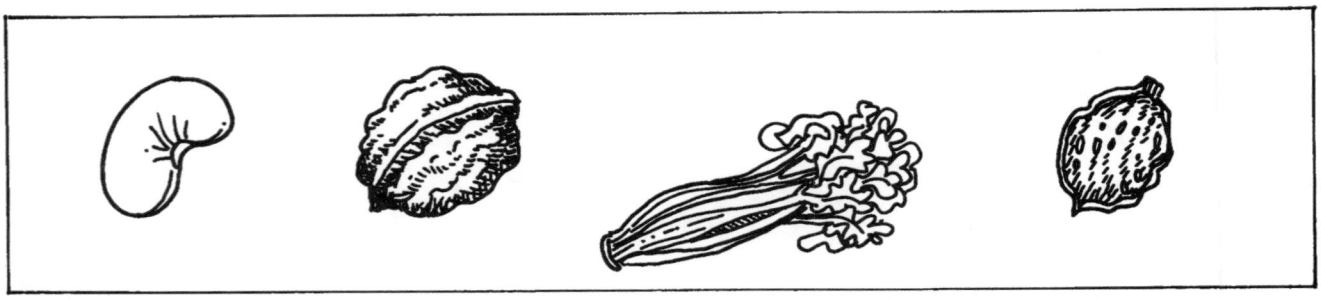

Make an X on the picture that is not a seed.

Make an X on the picture that is not a flower.

Name_____

 Copyright ©2001 by Incentive Publications, Inc., Nashville, TN.

Where Do Animals Come From?

Some animals are hatched from eggs.

Some mothers of babies hatched from eggs get food for their babies.

Others do not.

Draw a picture of another animal that hatches from an egg.

Name_____

 Copyright ©2001 by Incentive Publications, Inc., Nashville, TN.

Bird Nests and Eggs

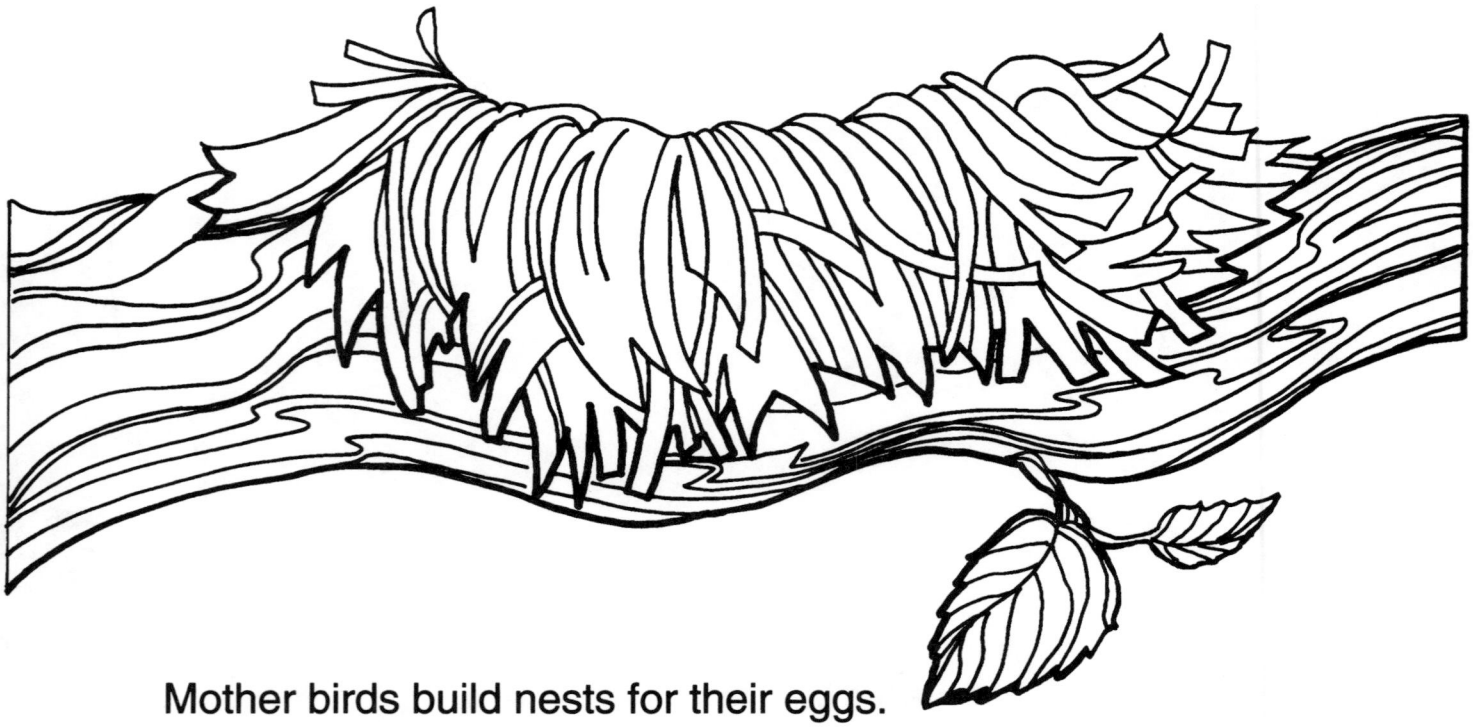

Mother birds build nests for their eggs.

The nest becomes the baby birds' first home.

Do you know what nests are made from?

Draw a mother bird and some baby birds in this nest.

Name_____

 Copyright ©2001 by Incentive Publications, Inc., Nashville, TN.

Mammals

Some animals are born alive.
Before birth they are carried inside their mothers.
Scientists use the word mammal for these animals.
All mammals have hair and feed their babies milk.

Cats are mammals.
Their babies are called kittens.

Draw two more kittens.

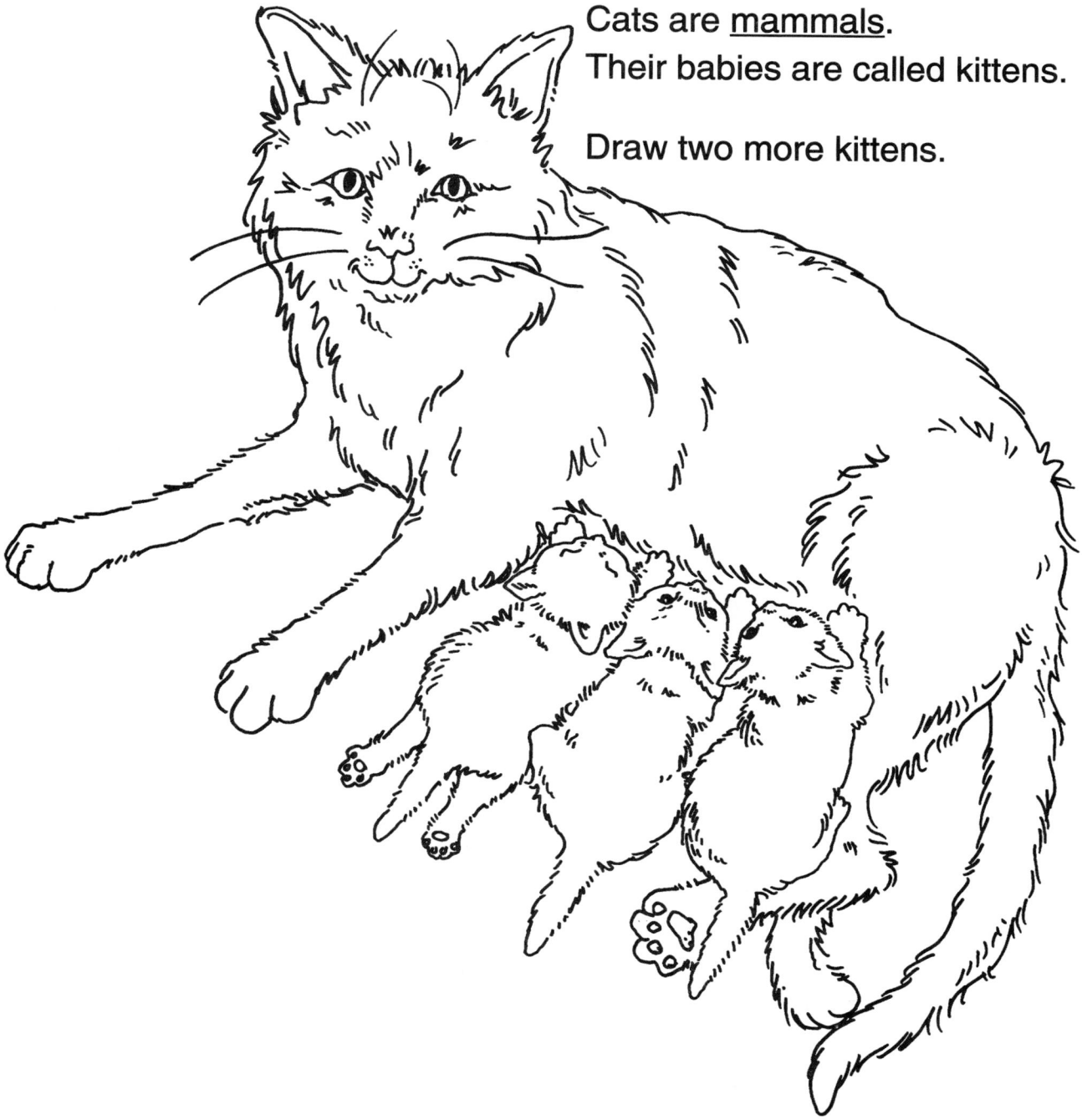

Name_____

Copyright ©2001 by Incentive Publications, Inc., Nashville, TN.

Self-Portrait

Did you know that you are a mammal?

Draw your picture here and write your name.

Name_____

 Copyright ©2001 by Incentive Publications, Inc., Nashville, TN.

Farm Animals

Here is a barn and a barnyard.

Draw some animals for the barnyard.

Can you tell what the farmer gets from each of the animals that you drew?

Name_____

Copyright ©2001 by Incentive Publications, Inc., Nashville, TN.

Pets

Pets are animals that live in homes with people.

Color the animals that would make good pets.

Make an X on the others.

Can you tell why an elephant would not make a good pet?

Name_____

 Copyright ©2001 by Incentive Publications, Inc., Nashville, TN.

A Special Pet

Draw a picture of a pet you would like to own.

Now, tell a story about the pet you drew.

Name_____

Copyright ©2001 by Incentive Publications, Inc., Nashville, TN.

Zoo Animals

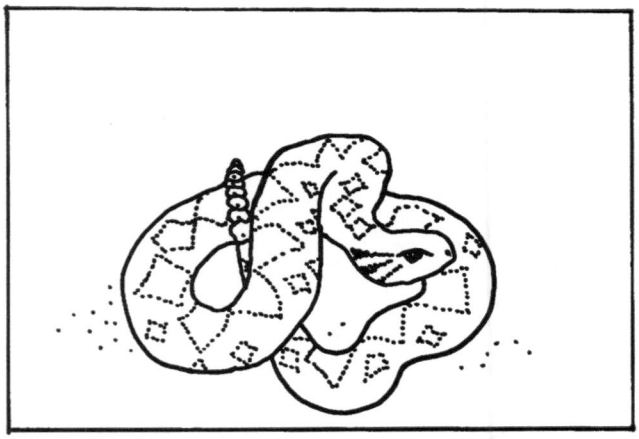

Some animals live in zoos.
The keeper tries to make the animal's new home as nearly like its old one as possible.

Draw a line from each animal to the picture of its natural home.
Say the name of each animal and the name of each home.

Name_____

Copyright ©2001 by Incentive Publications, Inc., Nashville, TN.

Insects

Insects are animals.

All insects have three main body parts and six legs.

Some insects are helpful to people.

Some insects are harmful to people.

Circle the insects.

Can you name them?

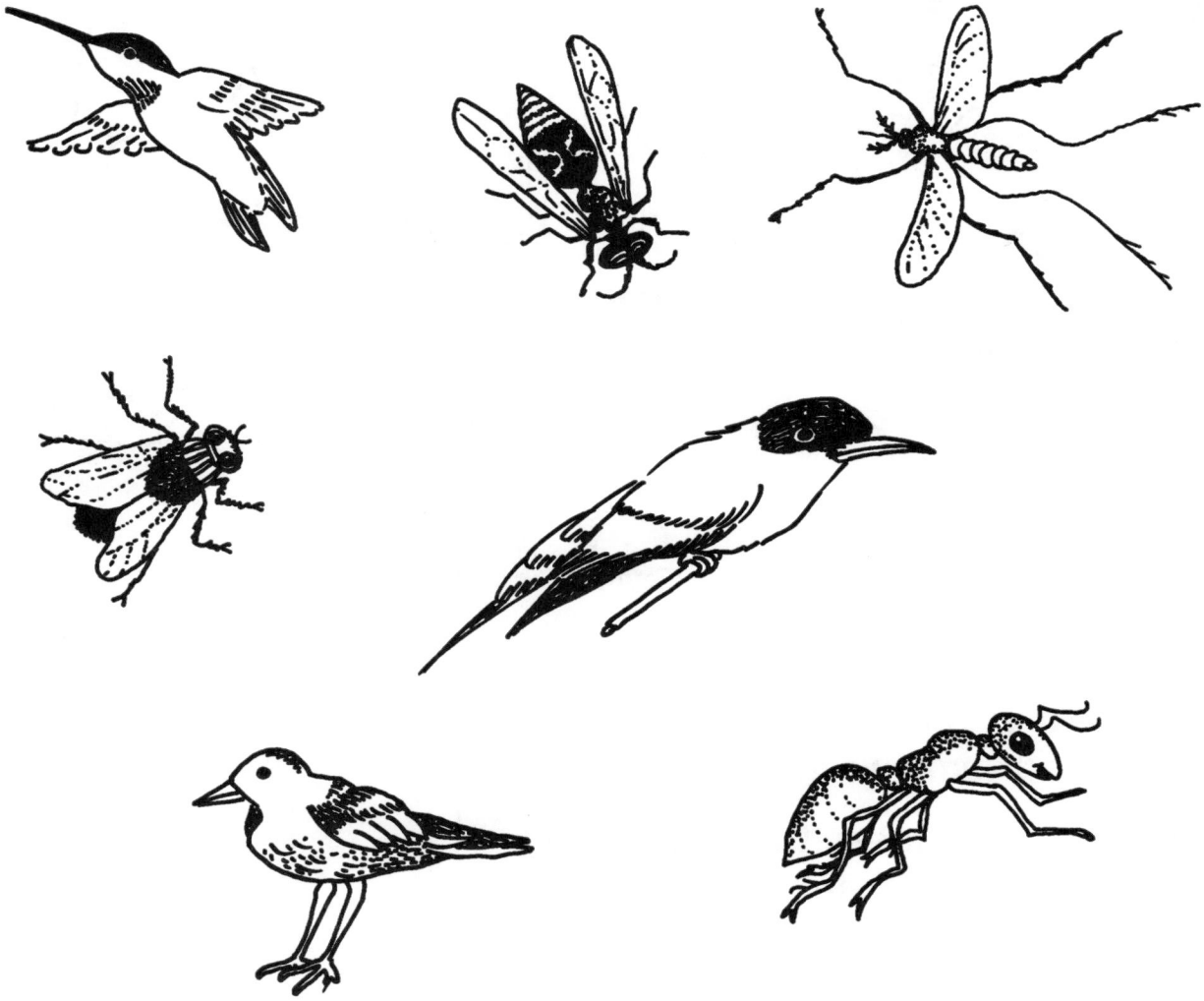

Name_____

Copyright ©2001 by Incentive Publications, Inc., Nashville, TN.

Animals on the Move

Animals move in different ways.

Some hop, some crawl, some swim, and some walk.

How many of these ways of moving have you observed?

Color the pictures of the animals that fly.

Draw a picture of an animal that swims.

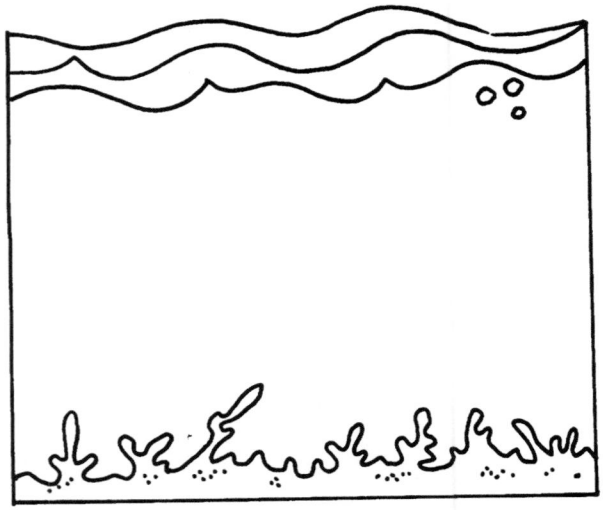

Name_____

Copyright ©2001 by Incentive Publications, Inc., Nashville, TN.

Dot-to-Dot, 1 to 30

Draw dot-to-dot to find an animal that eats both plants and other animals.

Name_____

Copyright ©2001 by Incentive Publications, Inc., Nashville, TN.

Turtles and Snails

Some animals use their coverings for protection.

Turtles pull their legs and heads into their shells if they are touched.

Snails can pull their whole bodies into their shells.

Have you ever touched a snail?

Color the snail shell.

Name_____

 Copyright ©2001 by Incentive Publications, Inc., Nashville, TN.

Animal Coverings

Animals have many different kinds of coverings.

Make an X on the animals that have feather coverings.

Color the pictures of the other animals.

How many of these animals can you name?

Name_____

 Copyright ©2001 by Incentive Publications, Inc., Nashville, TN.

Dinosaurs

Some very large animals that lived on the earth many years ago were called dinosaurs.

Say this big word. Write it.

dinosaurs

Can you tell why dinosaurs are not living today?
Color the picture.

Name_____

 Copyright ©2001 by Incentive Publications, Inc., Nashville, TN.

Habitats

Can you tell what the word habitat means?

A habitat is a home for living things.

Color pictures of the animals in their natural habitats.

Name_____

Copyright ©2001 by Incentive Publications, Inc., Nashville, TN.

Living Things Review

Plants and animals are living things.

They need each other to keep the balance of nature.

Make an X on the picture that is not a plant.

Make an X on the picture that is not an animal.

Make an X on the picture that is not a living thing.

Name_____

Copyright ©2001 by Incentive Publications, Inc., Nashville, TN.

Living Things Review

Use your blue crayon to color the animal that lives in the ocean.

Use your brown and yellow crayons to color the animal that lives in the jungle.

Use your green crayon to color the animal that lives in the desert.

Use your black crayon to color the animal that lives in the forest.

Name_____

 Copyright ©2001 by Incentive Publications, Inc., Nashville, TN.

Paste-Up

Cut out the pictures at the bottom of the page
and paste each one in its natural habitat.

Color the scene.

Copyright ©2001 by Incentive Publications, Inc., Nashville, TN.

The Human Body

Is Skin Just A Cover-Up?

All animals have some kind of covering on their bodies.
People have skin.
Skin is wonderful because it can do so many things.
Look at the skin on your body and think about these things.
Skin fits just perfectly.
It isn't too big or too little. It is just the right size.

Hold one hand in front of you.
Wiggle your fingers and watch the skin move.
Draw around your hand here.
Look at the skin on your hand as you draw.

Name_____

 Copyright ©2001 by Incentive Publications, Inc., Nashville, TN.

Temperature Control

Skin is waterproof!

If it weren't, you might soak up water in the bathtub!

Think about that the next time you take a bath.

Skin keeps you at just the right temperature.

It keeps your body warm when the weather is cold and lets you sweat to cool off when the weather is hot.

Draw a picture of yourself dressed for cold weather.

Name_____

Copyright ©2001 by Incentive Publications, Inc., Nashville, TN.

Skin Protection

Skin is thin where it needs to be — like on your eyelids — and thick in other places where you need more protection — like on the palms of your hands and the soles of your feet.

Skin protects you from germs, from hot sun, from lots of harmful things.

Feel the skin on your arms and legs. How does it feel?

Draw a picture of yourself dressed for hot weather.

Name_____

 Copyright ©2001 by Incentive Publications, Inc., Nashville, TN.

Freckles

Almost everyone has something under the skin called pigment.

Pigment is color.

When you are out in the sun, the sun makes some of the pigment come out on your skin, and you get a suntan.

Freckles are tiny spots on the skin where there is some extra pigment.

Some people get freckles, other people do not.

Draw freckles on one child's face.

Name_____

Copyright ©2001 by Incentive Publications, Inc., Nashville, TN.

Here are some faces for you to make freckles on . . .

Write the word freckles.

Write the word that tells what makes freckles.

pigment

Name_____

 Copyright ©2001 by Incentive Publications, Inc., Nashville, TN.

Virus

A wart is a little bump on your skin.

It doesn't hurt, and often it goes away by itself.

What else do you know about warts?

Scientists think that a virus on your skin may cause warts.

A virus is a germ. It is too tiny to see.

You will hear people talk about having a virus.

Write the word so you will remember it.

_____

virus

Name_____

Copyright ©2001 by Incentive Publications, Inc., Nashville, TN.

Skeleton

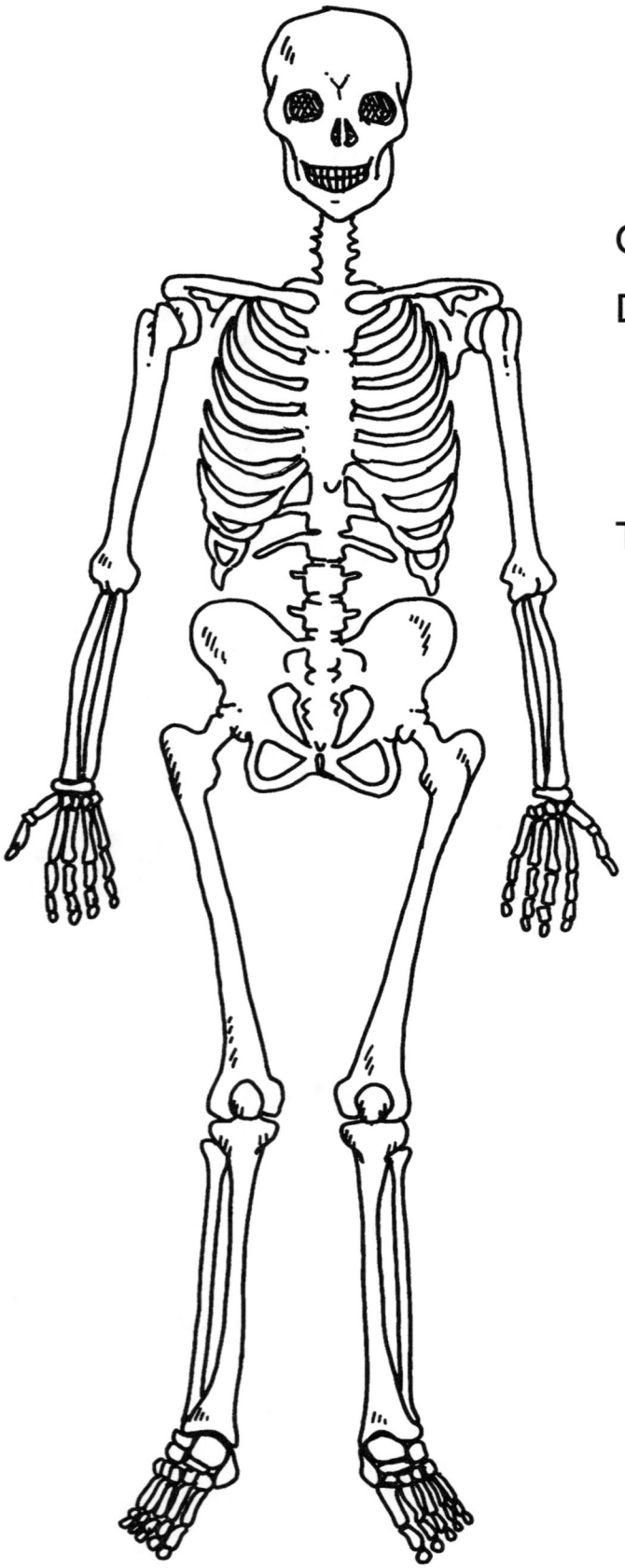

Ooooh! A skeleton!

Does it look scary?
Of course not!
Skeletons are not
scary at all.

Trace the skeleton with
your pencil.

Name_____

Copyright ©2001 by Incentive Publications, Inc., Nashville, TN.

Inside, Outside

Do you know that this is a picture of what you look like on the inside?

If you could take off your skin and wear just your bones, you would look something like this.

All your bones together are called your skeleton.

Color the skeleton.

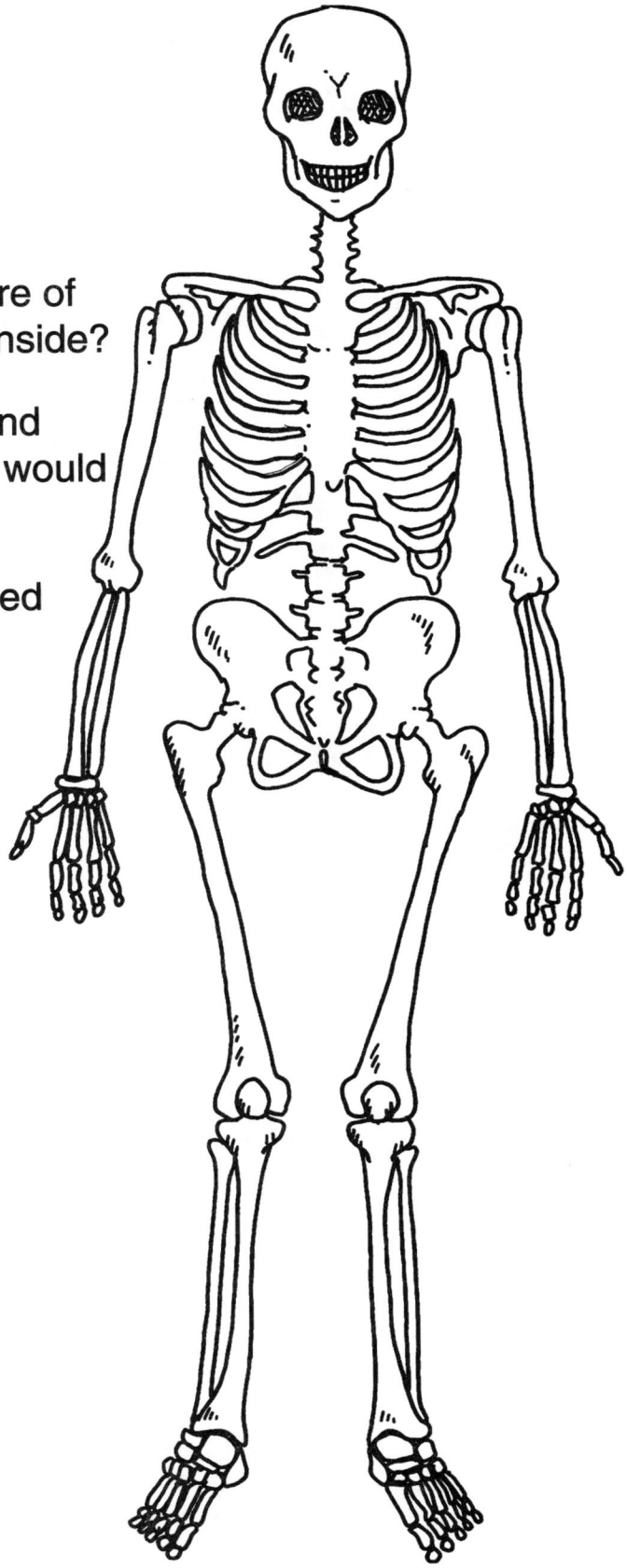

Name_____

Copyright ©2001 by Incentive Publications, Inc., Nashville, TN.

Body Parts

Wiggle your toes,
Scratch your head,
Bend your elbows,
Now, shake my hand!

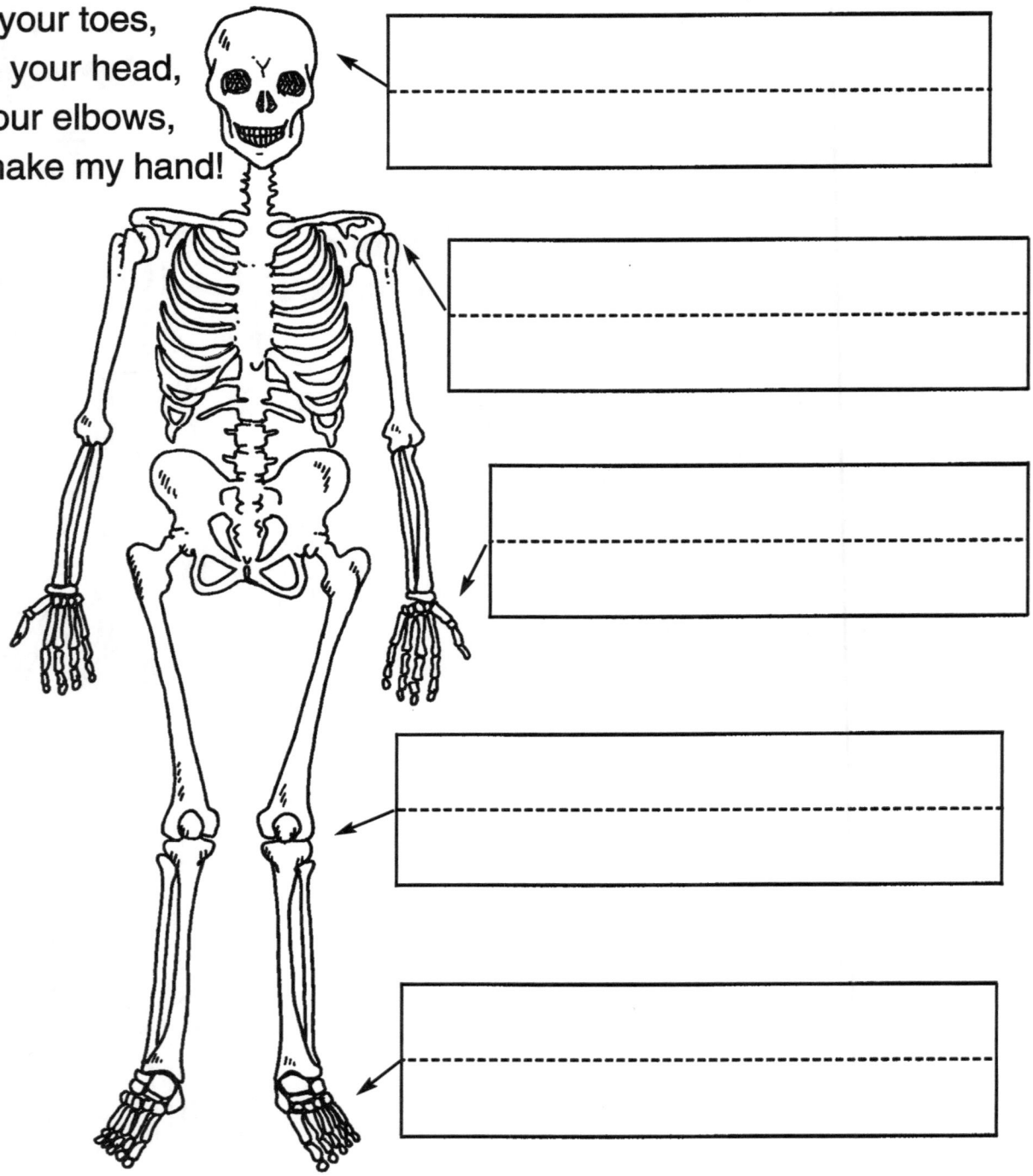

Look at this skeleton. Can you name the parts of the body which are pointed out by the arrows?

Use these words to help you label the parts of the body.

Head Foot Hand Knee Shoulder

Name_____

Copyright ©2001 by Incentive Publications, Inc., Nashville, TN.

Brain Power

What does this picture look like?
You might think it is a sponge.

Would you believe it is really a picture of a human brain?

Your brain is a very important part of your body because it tells all the other parts when and how to work.

Your finger or eye or hand or leg — no part of you can move until your brain tells it to move.

Write the name of this important part of your body.

brain

Name_____

Copyright ©2001 by Incentive Publications, Inc., Nashville, TN.

How Does Your Heart Beat?

We call this a heart

BUT

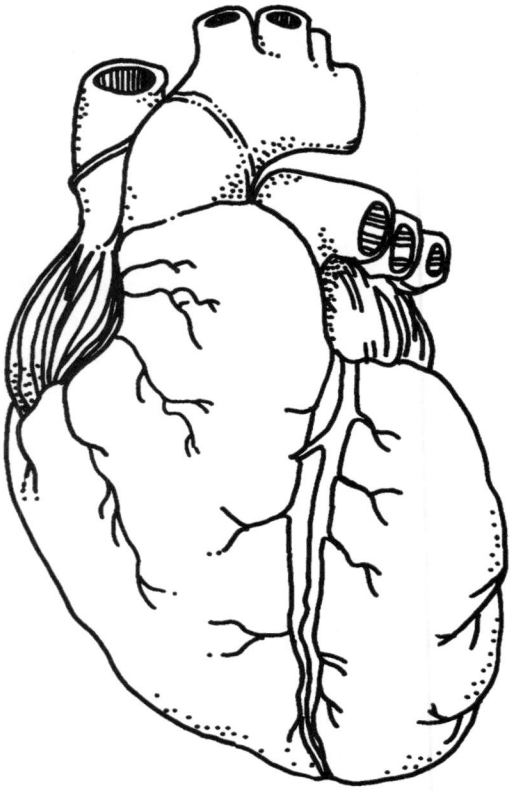

if we could see a human heart, it would look more like this.

The heart is a muscle.

It acts as a pump to move blood through the body. Each time it pumps, we can hear a heartbeat.

Your heart beats more than 100,000 times each day.

Have you ever listened to your heartbeat?

Write the word to help you remember this important muscle.

heart

Name_____

 Copyright ©2001 by Incentive Publications, Inc., Nashville, TN.

Count Your Pulse

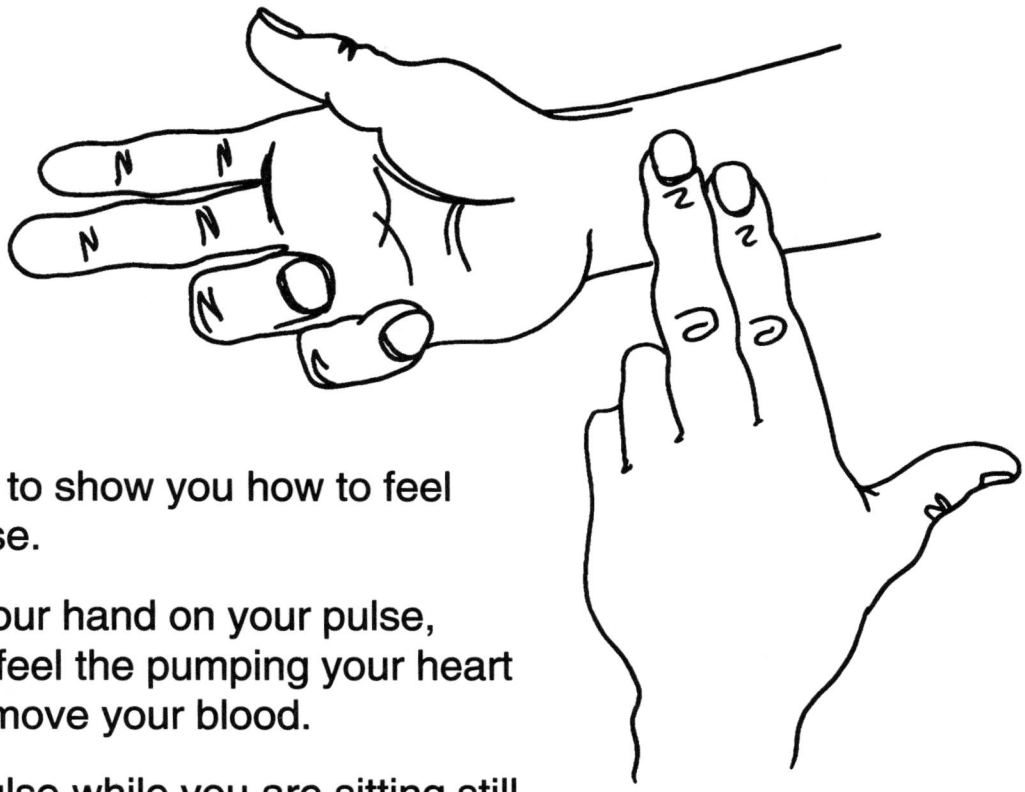

Ask someone to show you how to feel your pulse.

If you place your hand on your pulse, you can feel the pumping your heart does to move your blood.

Count your pulse while you are sitting still.

Then jump up and down several times.

Now count your pulse again.

What happens?

Why?

Name_____

 Copyright ©2001 by Incentive Publications, Inc., Nashville, TN.

Staying Well and Healthy

These pictures show some things human beings need to stay well and healthy.

Draw a picture of yourself doing something healthy.

Name_____

 Copyright ©2001 by Incentive Publications, Inc., Nashville, TN.

Taking Care of Your Body

Human beings need to take good care of their bodies so that all the parts of it will work right. Here are some pictures of things to do.

Draw a picture of yourself doing something to take care of your body.

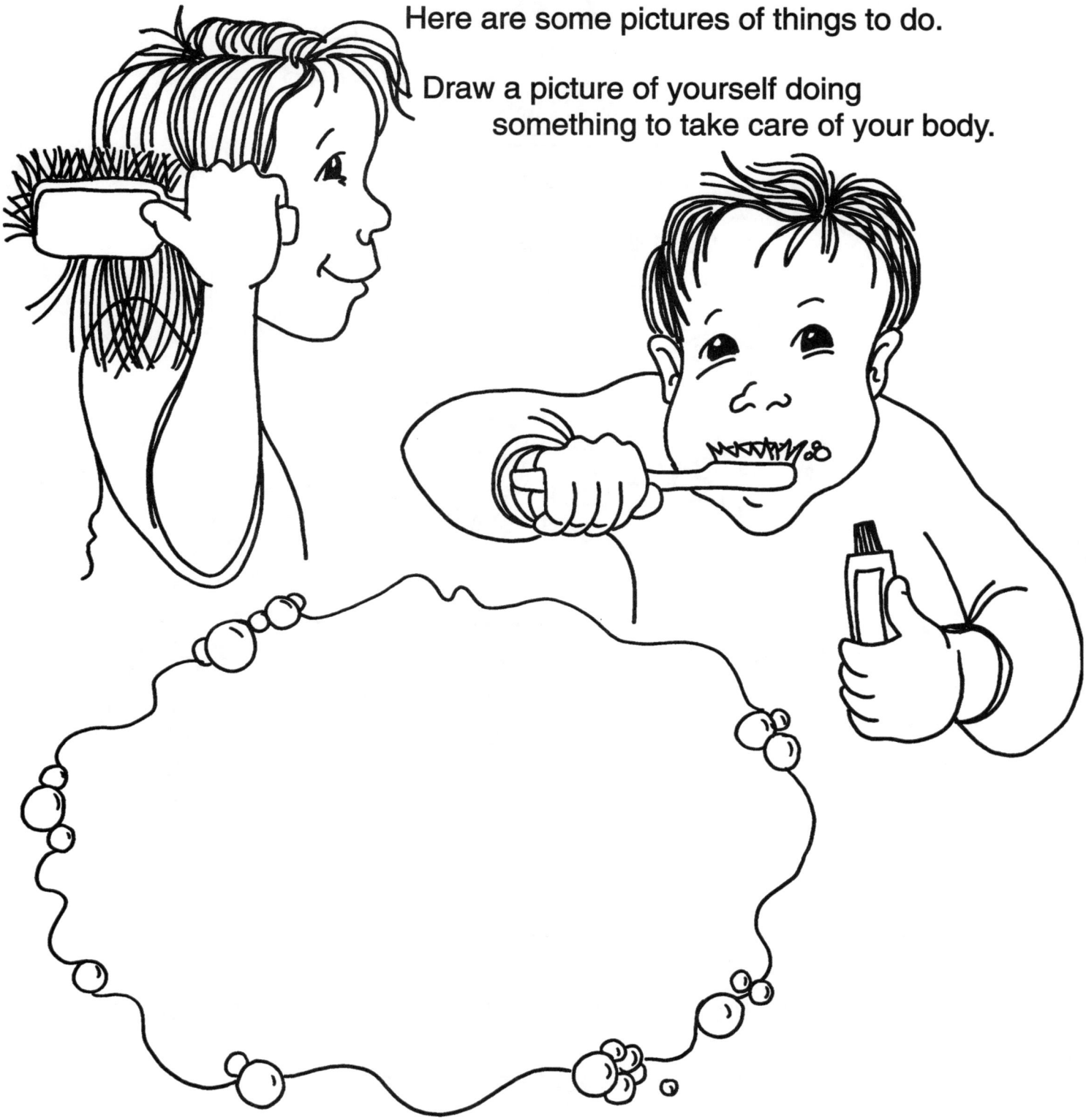

Name_____

Copyright ©2001 by Incentive Publications, Inc., Nashville, TN.

Good Food for a Good Body

Good food and regular eating habits are very important to the human body.

Did you eat some food from each of the main food groups yesterday?

Color the pictures and think about your own diet.

Name_____

 Copyright ©2001 by Incentive Publications, Inc., Nashville, TN.

Dinner Time

Draw pictures that show healthy, well-balanced lunches for each of these people.

Name_____

Copyright ©2001 by Incentive Publications, Inc., Nashville, TN.

Exercise Express

Do you know what happens to your body if you fail to get enough exercise?

Follow the dots to find one good way to exercise.

Then draw a picture of yourself exercising in your favorite way.

Name_____

 Copyright ©2001 by Incentive Publications, Inc., Nashville, TN.

Sleepy Time

Your body sleeps when it needs rest.

When it gets too tired to act the way it should, it needs to slow down.

When you sleep, all the working parts of your body work more slowly so they can rest.

Do you get enough rest?

Draw a picture of yourself in bed.

Name_____

Copyright ©2001 by Incentive Publications, Inc., Nashville, TN.

Do You Know Why People Yawn?

Sometimes when you're tired, you yawn.

Sometimes you yawn when you're not very tired.

Your body just needs some fresh air.

When you yawn, you get a big gulp of fresh air and breathe out a big gulp of air.

Draw a picture of yourself yawning.

Name_____

Copyright ©2001 by Incentive Publications, Inc., Nashville, TN.

Ahh-choo!!

Here is a poem about sneezes.

Say it.

Teach it to a friend.

It's fun to do!

Sneezes

Sneezle . . . bambeezle . . . bumbozzle . . . KER-CHOO!
You can't choose to sneeze
It just happens to you!
You can hop, you can flop,
But there's no way to stop
A sneezle . . . bambeezle . . . bumbozzle . . . KER-CHOO!

What happens to make you sneeze?

Sneezes sneak up on you, and you can't do much about them but let them come out.

You sneeze when something gets inside your nose that doesn't belong there. It may be a piece of dust or dirt. It tickles the nerves in your nose and makes you sneeze to blow out the dirt.

Name_____

Copyright ©2001 by Incentive Publications, Inc., Nashville, TN.

Hot or Cold

When it's hot, your body sweats through tiny openings in the skin called pores.

When it's cold, those pores close up. And when you get very cold, the muscles in your body wiggle all by themselves to warm you up.

That's what shivering is.

Draw a picture of a shivering puppy.

Name_____

Copyright ©2001 by Incentive Publications, Inc., Nashville, TN.

Hiccups

Is it hard to hiccup?

Whoops! No!

It's hard to stop!

Do you know what makes you hiccup?

When you breathe, a muscle called your diaphragm pushes and pulls the air in and out of your lungs.

Sometimes your diaphragm jerks. When it does, it pushes a puff of air out past your voice box and makes you "hic."

No one knows a sure way to stop hiccups.

People try lots of things.

Sometimes taking a long drink of water helps.

Have you ever tried to stop hiccups? How did you do it?

Write the word and try to remember what causes hiccups.

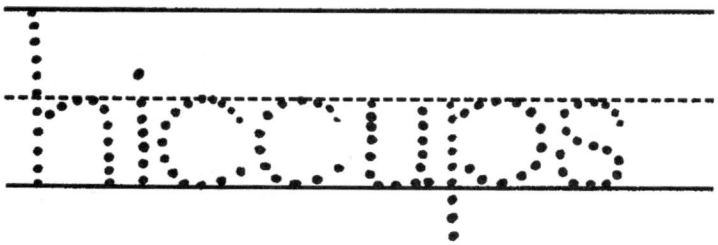

Name_____

Copyright ©2001 by Incentive Publications, Inc., Nashville, TN.

How Does a Body Fix Itself?

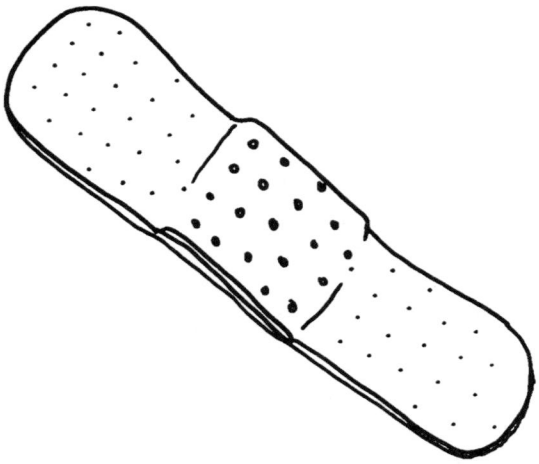

The body of an animal is one of only a few things that can fix itself when it gets hurt.

When you cut your finger, you clean it, put a bandage on it, and . . .

ABRACADABRA!

Like magic, when you take off the bandage several days later, the cut has healed.

Just a little more time, and you might not be able to see where the cut was at all.

AMAZING!

But how does the body do it?

Name_____

 Copyright ©2001 by Incentive Publications, Inc., Nashville, TN.

How Cuts Heal

As soon as you cut your finger, it begins to bleed.

Tiny cells and fibers in the blood begin to stick together to make the blood thicken.

Finally the blood gets hard and makes a cover—a scab—on the cut.

The scab protects the cut while other cells work under and inside the skin to heal the cut.

When the cut is healed, the scab falls off!

WOW!

Name_____

 Copyright ©2001 by Incentive Publications, Inc., Nashville, TN.

Living, Growing, and Changing

You are a living and growing thing.

Your body is changing all the time.

Draw a picture that shows how you think you will look ten years from now.

Try to think about how tall you will be, how your hair will look, and how your face will change.

Name_____

 Copyright ©2001 by Incentive Publications, Inc., Nashville, TN.

Earth and Sky

Exploring

Be an explorer!

Take a walk outside. Look for living things.

Maybe you will see a butterfly or a spider web.

If you are lucky, you might hear a mockingbird sing
or smell honeysuckle in bloom.

Color all the living things in this picture.

Name_____

 Copyright ©2001 by Incentive Publications, Inc., Nashville, TN.

Did You Know That the Earth is Round?

It is covered with water, soil, rock, plants, and animals.

The shapes show where the land is.

The rest is water.

Color everything except the shapes blue.

Name_____

 Copyright ©2001 by Incentive Publications, Inc., Nashville, TN.

Water, Water, Water

Did you notice that you colored more than half of the Earth blue?

That is because most of the Earth is covered with water.

Can you think of some plants and animals that live in water and could not live on land?

Draw a picture of two things that live only in water.

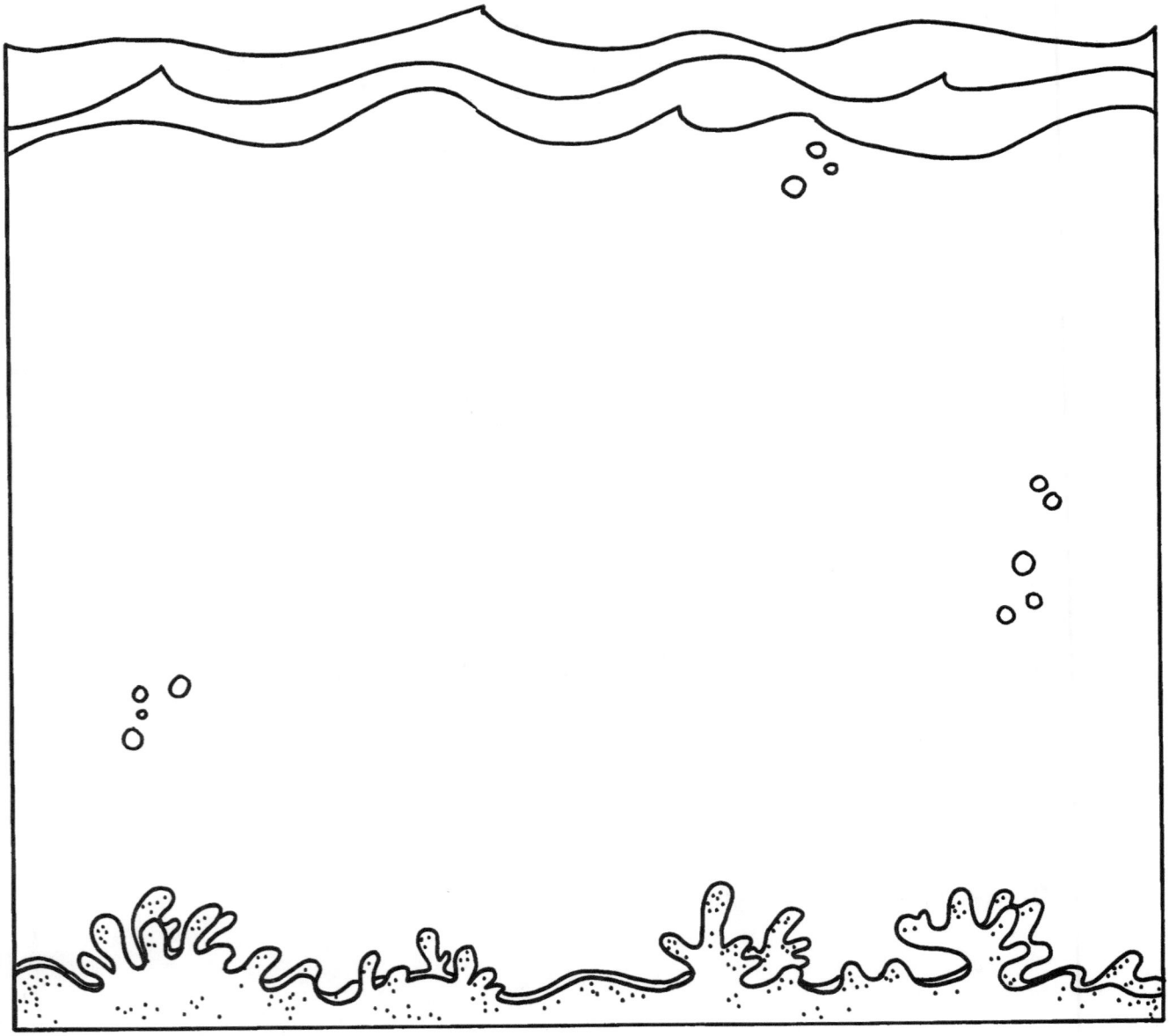

Name_____

 Copyright ©2001 by Incentive Publications, Inc., Nashville, TN.

What Makes Day and Night?

The Earth is turning slowly all the time.

As the part we live on turns toward the sun, we have day.

As it turns away from the sun, we have night.

Do you know how long it takes the Earth to make one full turn?

Color the sun yellow.

Name_____

 Copyright ©2001 by Incentive Publications, Inc., Nashville, TN.

Night and Day

Use your crayons to make this a daytime picture.

Use your crayons to make this a nighttime picture.

Name_____

 Copyright ©2001 by Incentive Publications, Inc., Nashville, TN.

For Use at Night

Here are two things you would use only at night.

Draw a picture of one more thing that you would use when it is dark.

Color the pictures.

Name_____

Copyright ©2001 by Incentive Publications, Inc., Nashville, TN.

For Use During Daylight Hours

These two things would be used during daylight hours.

Draw a picture of one more thing you would use when the sun is shining.

Add the sun to the picture.

Name_____

 Copyright ©2001 by Incentive Publications, Inc., Nashville, TN.

My Favorite Season

Spring, summer, winter, fall, I like _____ best of all!

Draw a picture here to show the season you like best.

Use three crayons to color the picture.

Name_____

Copyright ©2001 by Incentive Publications, Inc., Nashville, TN.

What Makes Summer and Winter?

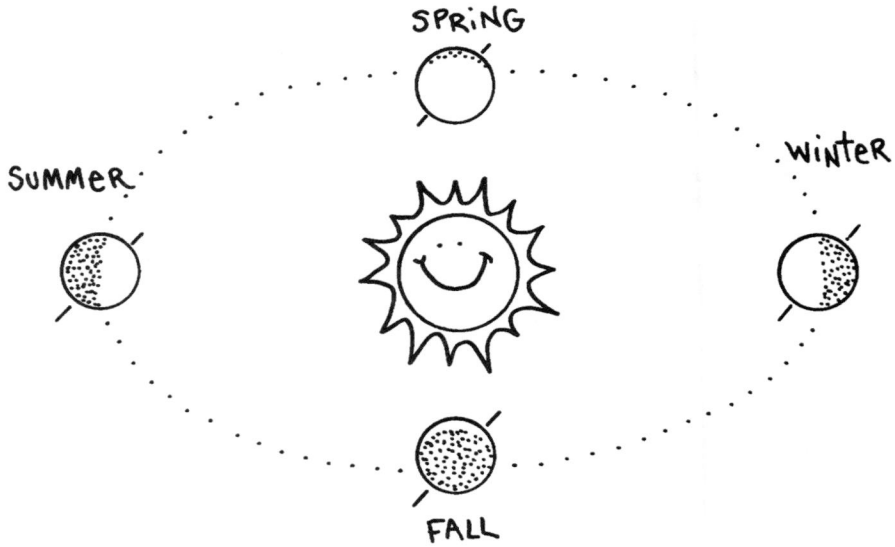

The Earth is tilted or slanted toward the sun so that the sun shines on it more directly at some times than at others.

When it is summer, the sun shines directly on the Earth.

When the sun's rays are not very direct, it is winter.

Spring and fall are in between.

Write the names of the four seasons.

spring

summer

fall

winter

Name_____

 Copyright ©2001 by Incentive Publications, Inc., Nashville, TN.

Four Seasons

Color the pictures.

Name_____

Copyright ©2001 by Incentive Publications, Inc., Nashville, TN.

Seasons in Living Color

Use all your crayons to make each picture show a different season.

Name_____

 Copyright ©2001 by Incentive Publications, Inc., Nashville, TN.

What Do You Know About the Sun?

The sun is a star.

It looks so-o-o big because it is the star nearest the Earth.

It is a daytime star.

Draw a picture of something you like to do when the sun is shining brightly.

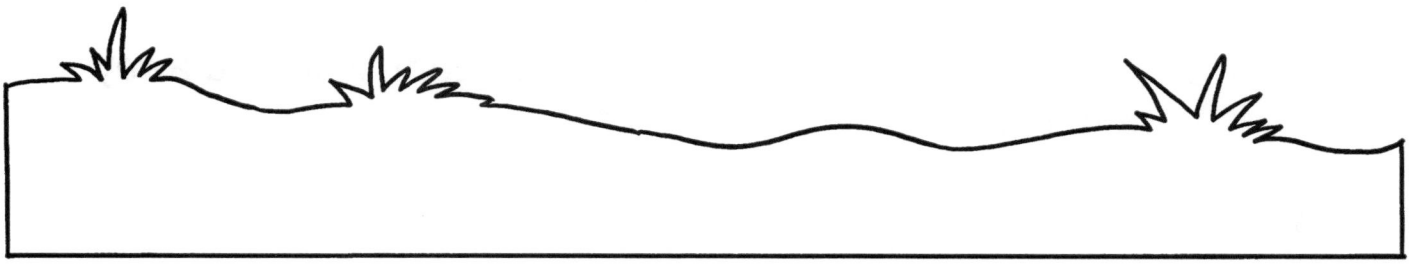

Name_____

Copyright ©2001 by Incentive Publications, Inc., Nashville, TN.

Stars

The stars we see at night are shining in the daytime, too.

We cannot see them until our part of the Earth is turned away from the sun. Can you tell why?

Draw some more stars.

Draw yourself in the picture.

Name_____

Copyright ©2001 by Incentive Publications, Inc., Nashville, TN.

Have You Ever Wished Upon a Star?

Write your wish here.

Name_____

Copyright ©2001 by Incentive Publications, Inc., Nashville, TN.

Moon Walk

Scientists have learned a lot about the moon by sending cameras inside space capsules to take pictures of it.

One of the things we have learned is that the moon has no wind or clouds.

We know, too, that the moon is hard to walk on.

Can you tell how we know this?

Color the nighttime sky blue. Color the moon and stars yellow.

Name_____

 Copyright ©2001 by Incentive Publications, Inc., Nashville, TN.

Space Visit

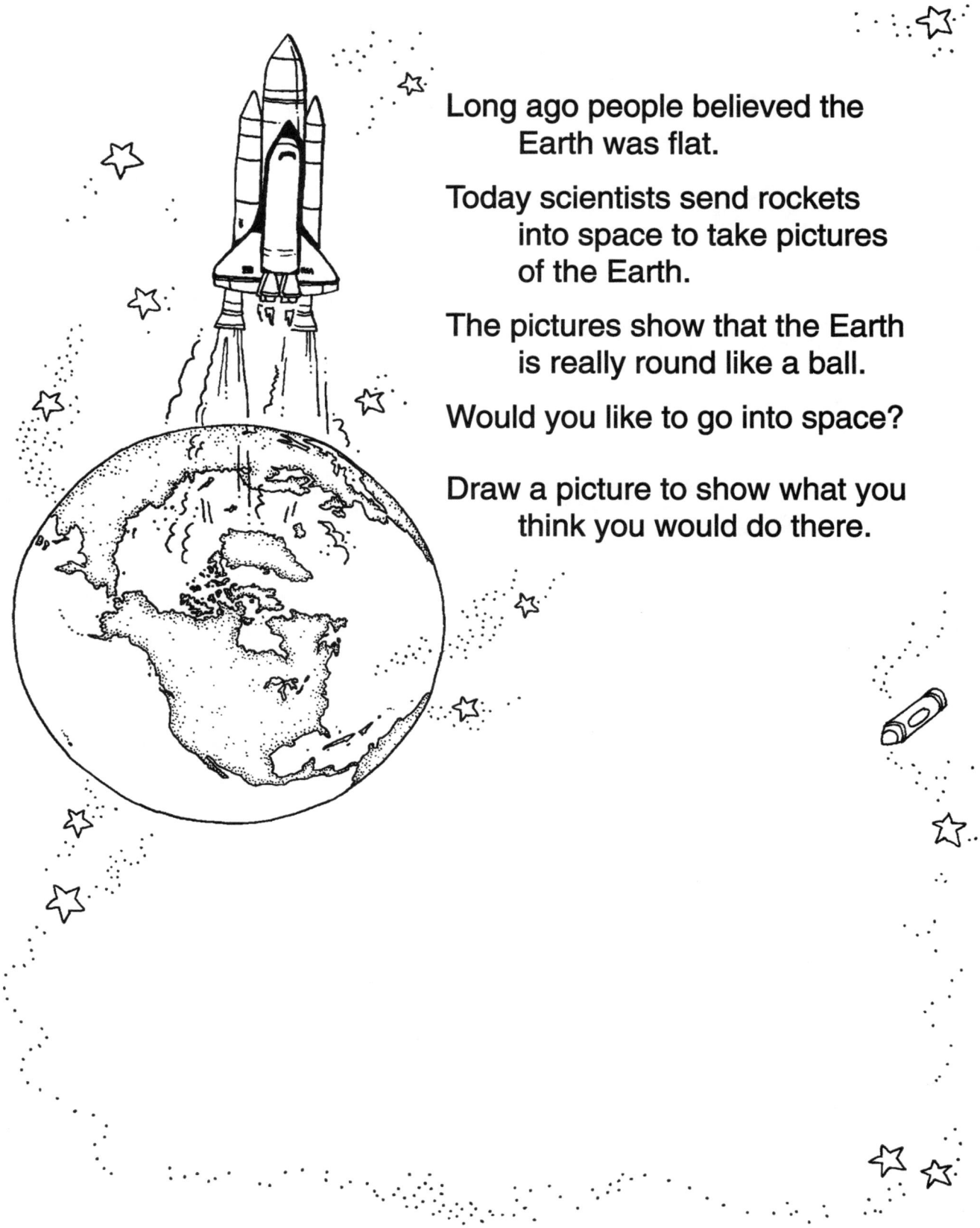

Long ago people believed the Earth was flat.

Today scientists send rockets into space to take pictures of the Earth.

The pictures show that the Earth is really round like a ball.

Would you like to go into space?

Draw a picture to show what you think you would do there.

Name_____

Copyright ©2001 by Incentive Publications, Inc., Nashville, TN.

Space Ship

Finish this picture to show how you think a spaceship you might travel in would look.

Add three things to the picture that you would take into space with you.

Name_____

 Copyright ©2001 by Incentive Publications, Inc., Nashville, TN.

Do You Know How Sand is Made?

A sandy beach is made of many tiny rocks.

These tiny rocks that we call sand have been broken down from big rocks by water and wind.

It takes many, many years for this to happen.

Draw a picture of a sandy beach here.

Put yourself in the picture.

Name_____

 Copyright ©2001 by Incentive Publications, Inc., Nashville, TN.

Rock-A-Round

Long ago the Earth was covered with big rocks.

Over the years, wind and water have broken many of these big rocks into smaller rocks.

We can still find many large rocks if we look for them.

Draw a picture of the largest rock you can remember seeing.
Where did you see it?

Name_____

 Copyright ©2001 by Incentive Publications, Inc., Nashville, TN.

Rocks of Long Ago

Did you know that you can learn about plants and animals that lived long ago by studying certain kinds of stones?

Some rocks have dents or prints made by animals or plants that lived and died long ago.

These dents or prints are called <u>fossils</u>.

Write this word so you will remember it.

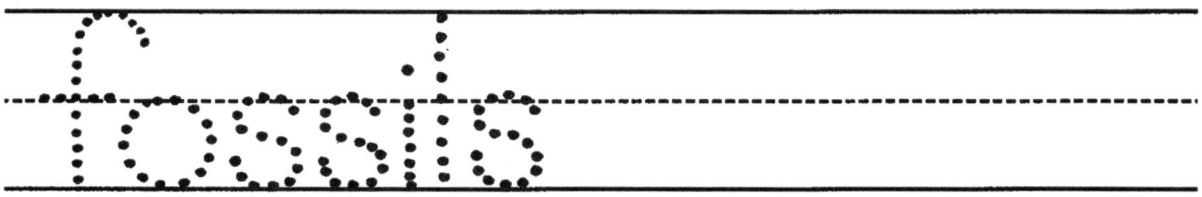

Name_____

 Copyright ©2001 by Incentive Publications, Inc., Nashville, TN.

Studying Rocks

A rockhound is someone who collects and studies rocks.

Look at different kinds of rocks.

Draw a picture of the most interesting rock in the collection.

MY MOST INTERESTING ROCK ☆ MY MOST INTERESTING ROCK ☆ MY MOST INTERESTING ROCK ☆ MY MOST INTERESTING ROCK ☆ MY MOST INTERESTING ROCK ☆

Name_____

Copyright ©2001 by Incentive Publications, Inc., Nashville, TN.

Air and Water

Air is Everywhere . . .

Can you see air?

Can you feel it?

Can you hear it?

Air is everywhere.

It is all around you.

Put your arms out straight and whirl around.

Did you feel the air as it rushed past you?

Draw a picture of yourself whirling around and feeling the air.

Name_____

 Copyright ©2001 by Incentive Publications, Inc., Nashville, TN.

Experiment with Air

1. Find a drinking straw.
   Blow through the straw
   onto your hand.
   Blow through the straw
   into a glass of water.

   Can you feel air?

   Can you see air?

2. Blow up a balloon.
   Let it drop.
   What happened?
   What pushed the balloon
   around and around?

3. Put an empty soda pop
   bottle in a big pan of water.
   Watch the bubbles
   come up.

   What made the bubbles?

Name_____

Copyright ©2001 by Incentive Publications, Inc., Nashville, TN.

. . . More Experiments

4. Place an empty juice can on a table. Try to blow it over.

   Can you do it?

   Now . . . fasten a balloon to the end of a drinking straw. Lay the balloon on the table and place the can on top of it. Blow through the straw into the balloon.

   What happened to the can?

Now can you answer these questions?

Where is air?

Can you see it?

Can you feel it?

Can you hear it?

Name_____

 Copyright ©2001 by Incentive Publications, Inc., Nashville, TN.

Living Things Need Clean Air

It is important for all living things to have clean, fresh air in which to live and grow.

When plants and animals live in unclean air, they become unhealthy.

We call unclean air polluted air.

Color the picture that shows clean, fresh air.

Name_____

 Copyright ©2001 by Incentive Publications, Inc., Nashville, TN.

X-Out Litter

People sometimes cause pollution by throwing empty bottles, boxes, and other waste materials into the yard or along the roadside.

This type of pollution is called <u>littering</u>.

Take a walk around your house or school to see how much litter you can find.

Maybe you can ask the people you know to stop polluting the space you live in.

Make an X on signs of pollution.

Color the rest of the picture.

Name_____

 Copyright ©2001 by Incentive Publications, Inc., Nashville, TN.

X-Out Air Pollution

Make an X on the things that cause air pollution.

Color the other three pictures.

Name_____

Copyright ©2001 by Incentive Publications, Inc., Nashville, TN.

Pollution Prevention

Draw a picture of something you can do to help prevent pollution.

Name_____

 Copyright ©2001 by Incentive Publications, Inc., Nashville, TN.

Color the Rainbow

When the sun shines right away after a shower, there is often a rainbow in the sky.

This rainbow has six colors.

The colors in the rainbow are red, orange, yellow, green, blue, and violet.

Color the rainbow.

Name_____

 Copyright ©2001 by Incentive Publications, Inc., Nashville, TN.

Evaporation

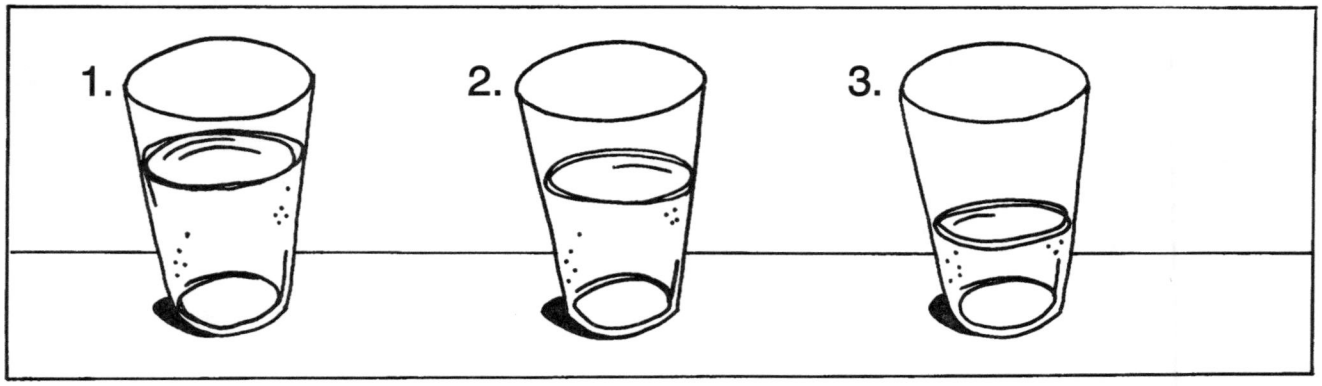

These pictures tell a story about water.

They tell what happens to water if it stands open to the air for a long time.

Picture 1 shows a glass of water almost full.

Picture 2 shows the glass the next day. Some water has disappeared.

Picture 3 shows that even more water has disappeared on the third day.

Where did the water go?

The water has gone up into the air!

Whenever water changes into vapor and goes up into the air, we say it evaporates.

What a big word!

Fill a glass almost full of water.

Mark the top of the water with a rubber band or a piece of tape.

Let the glass sit for several days.

Each day, look at the water to see what has happened.Does a little water disappear each day?

Name_____

 Copyright ©2001 by Incentive Publications, Inc., Nashville, TN.

Is Dissolving the Same as Disappearing?

1. Here is a small glass of water.

2. Put a spoonful of sugar in it.

3. Now we'll stir it.

4. Take out the spoon and look at the water. Can you see the sugar? What happened to it?

5. It seems to have disappeared. But if we taste the water, it will taste sweet. So we know the sugar is still there. We say it has dissolved.

Can you say the word <u>dissolve</u>?

Write it.

dissolve

Name_____

Copyright ©2001 by Incentive Publications, Inc., Nashville, TN.

An Experiment with Water and Ice

Put some ice cubes in a glass.

Try to cover the ice cubes with water. Whoops! They won't stay under the water. They keep coming up. They float on top of the water.

Do you know why?

Ice cubes float on water because they are lighter than water.

What other things float in water?

Perhaps you can try some objects in a bowl of water.

Name_____

 Copyright ©2001 by Incentive Publications, Inc., Nashville, TN.

Machines, Magnets, and Electricity

How Do Tools Make Hard Work Easy?

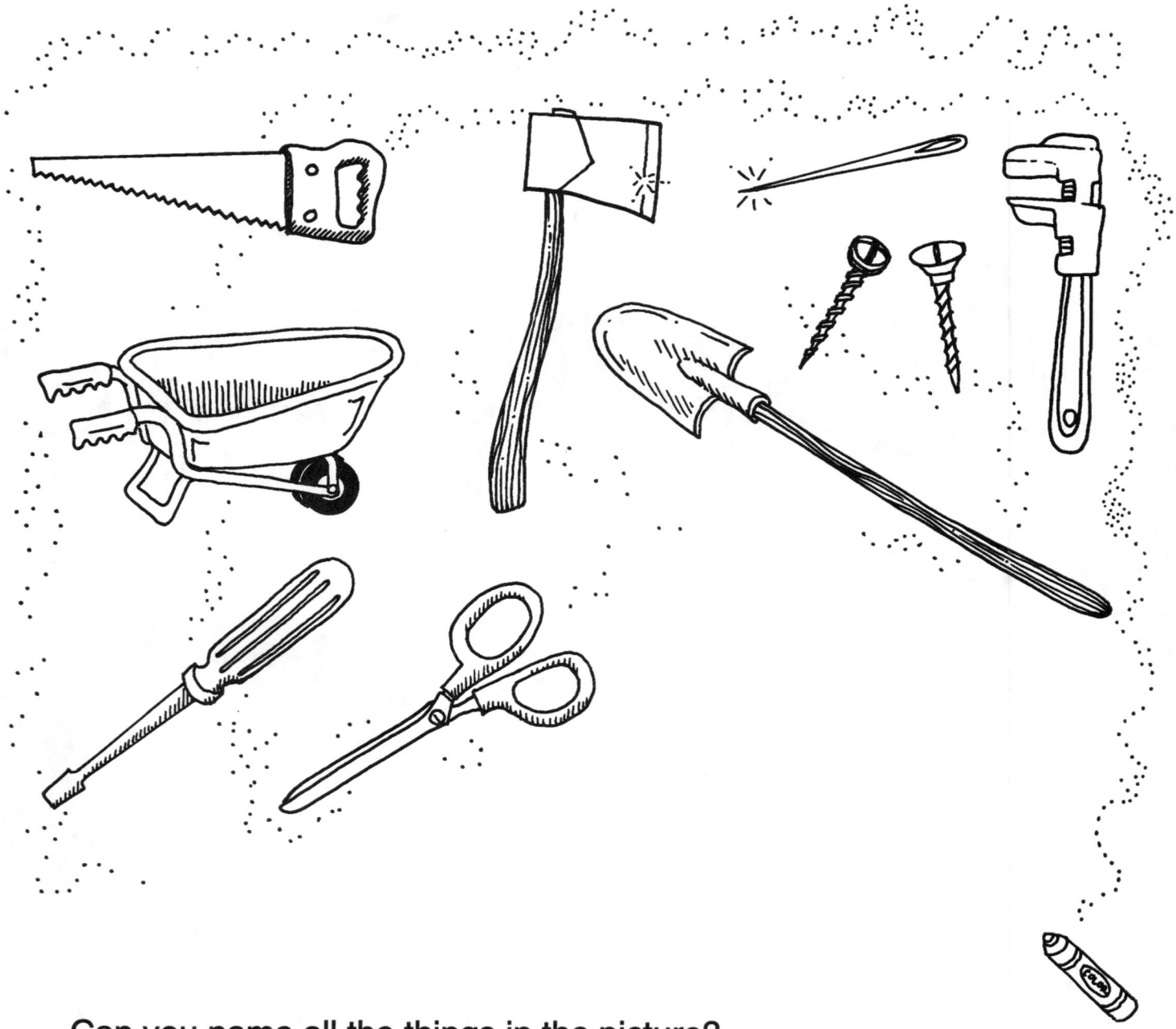

Can you name all the things in the picture?

Can you tell how each is used?

All these things are called tools.

Tools are simple machines that people use to make work easier.

Draw a picture of one other tool that you use at home or at school.

Name_____

 Copyright ©2001 by Incentive Publications, Inc., Nashville, TN.

Wheels

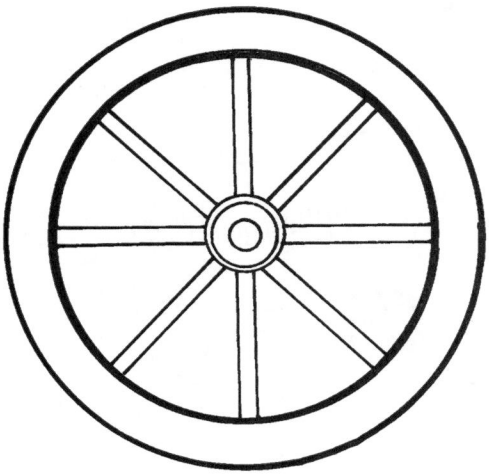

This is a wheel.

It is a machine that helps people.

It would be very hard to ride a bicycle or drive a car without wheels.

Color the picture that shows how wheels help people move.

Name_____

 Copyright ©2001 by Incentive Publications, Inc., Nashville, TN.

Wheels at Work

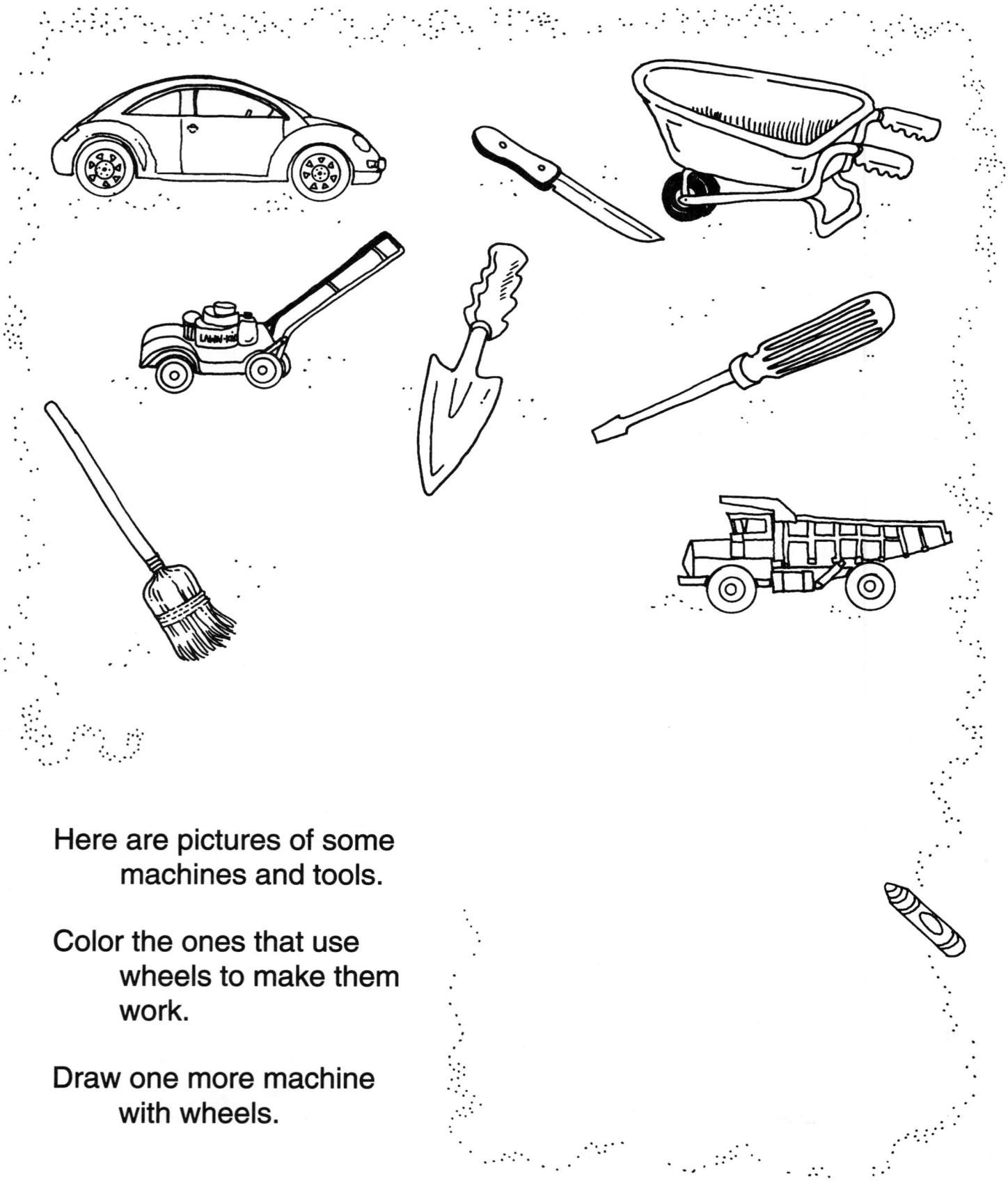

Here are pictures of some machines and tools.

Color the ones that use wheels to make them work.

Draw one more machine with wheels.

Name_____

 Copyright ©2001 by Incentive Publications, Inc., Nashville, TN.

Farm Tools

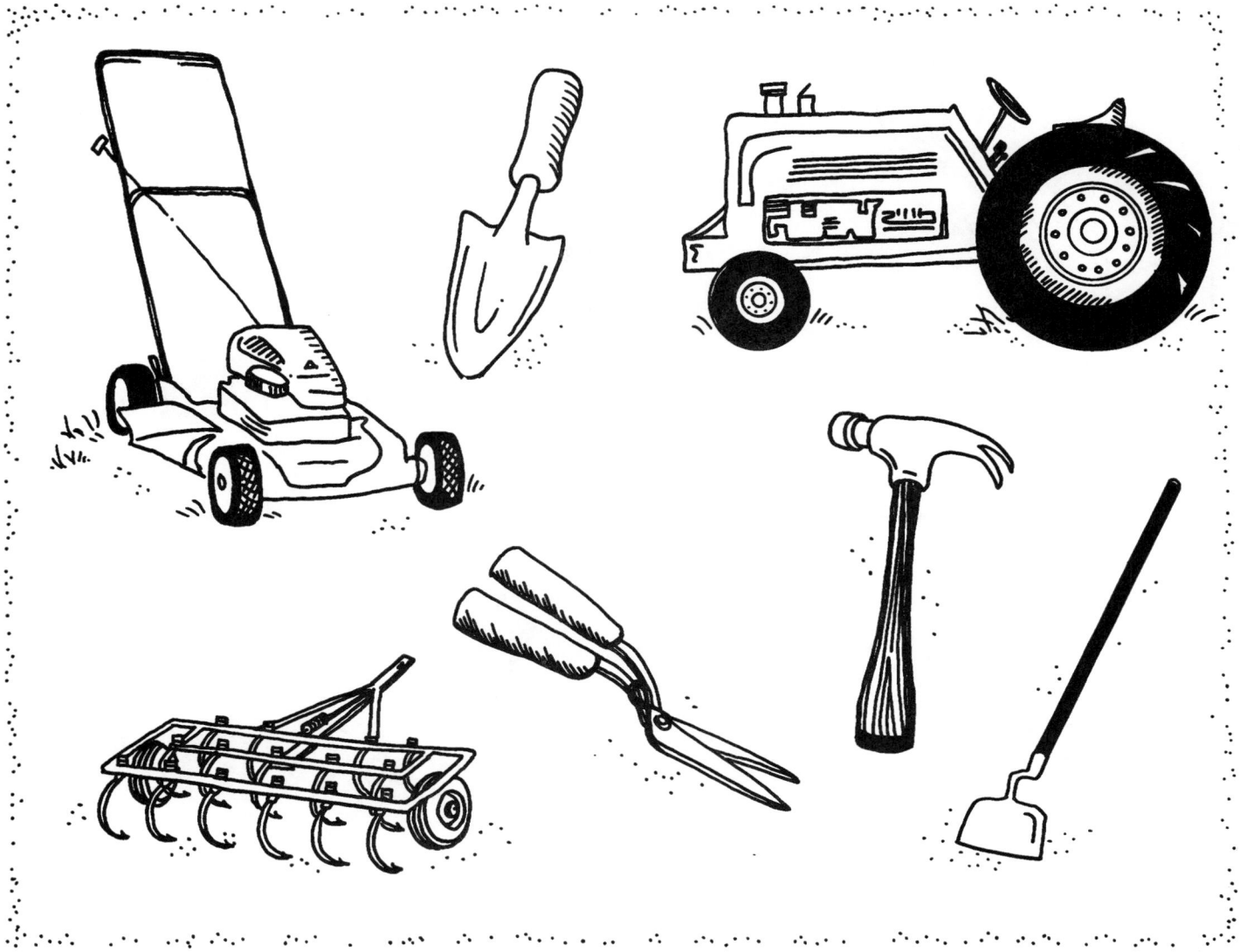

Different kinds of tools and machines are used to care for plants.

Make an X on the tools and machines that a farmer uses in the fields.

Do you know the names of all these tools and machines?

Name_____

 Copyright ©2001 by Incentive Publications, Inc., Nashville, TN.

Tools That Help Care for Plants

Draw a circle around the picture of the tool that would be used to care for plants.

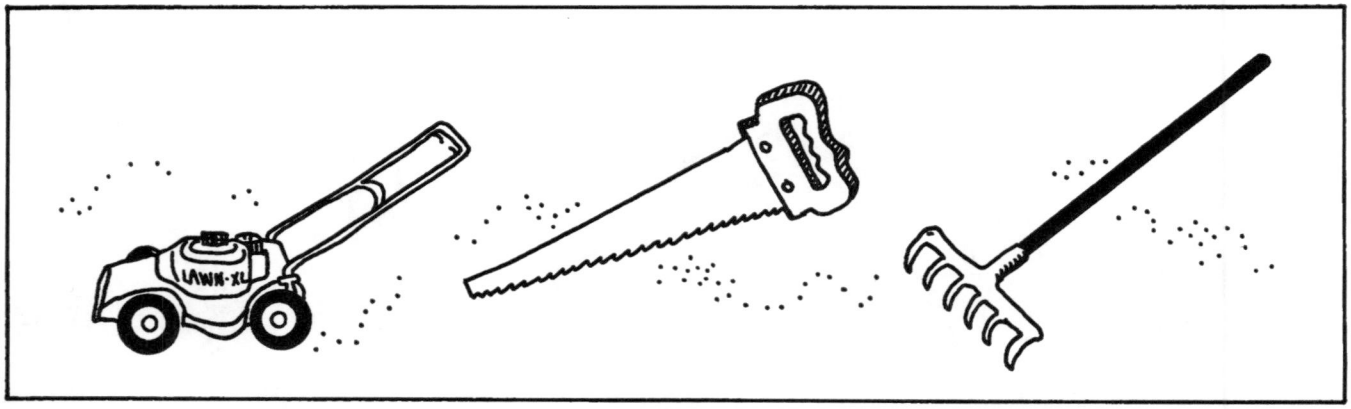

Make an X on the picture of the tool that would not be used to care for plants.

Draw a picture of a tool being used to care for plants.

Name_____

 Copyright ©2001 by Incentive Publications, Inc., Nashville, TN.

What Do You Think?

Do you think one small girl can balance two boys on a seesaw?

Yes, it is possible because she has a lever to help her.

The seesaw is a lever.

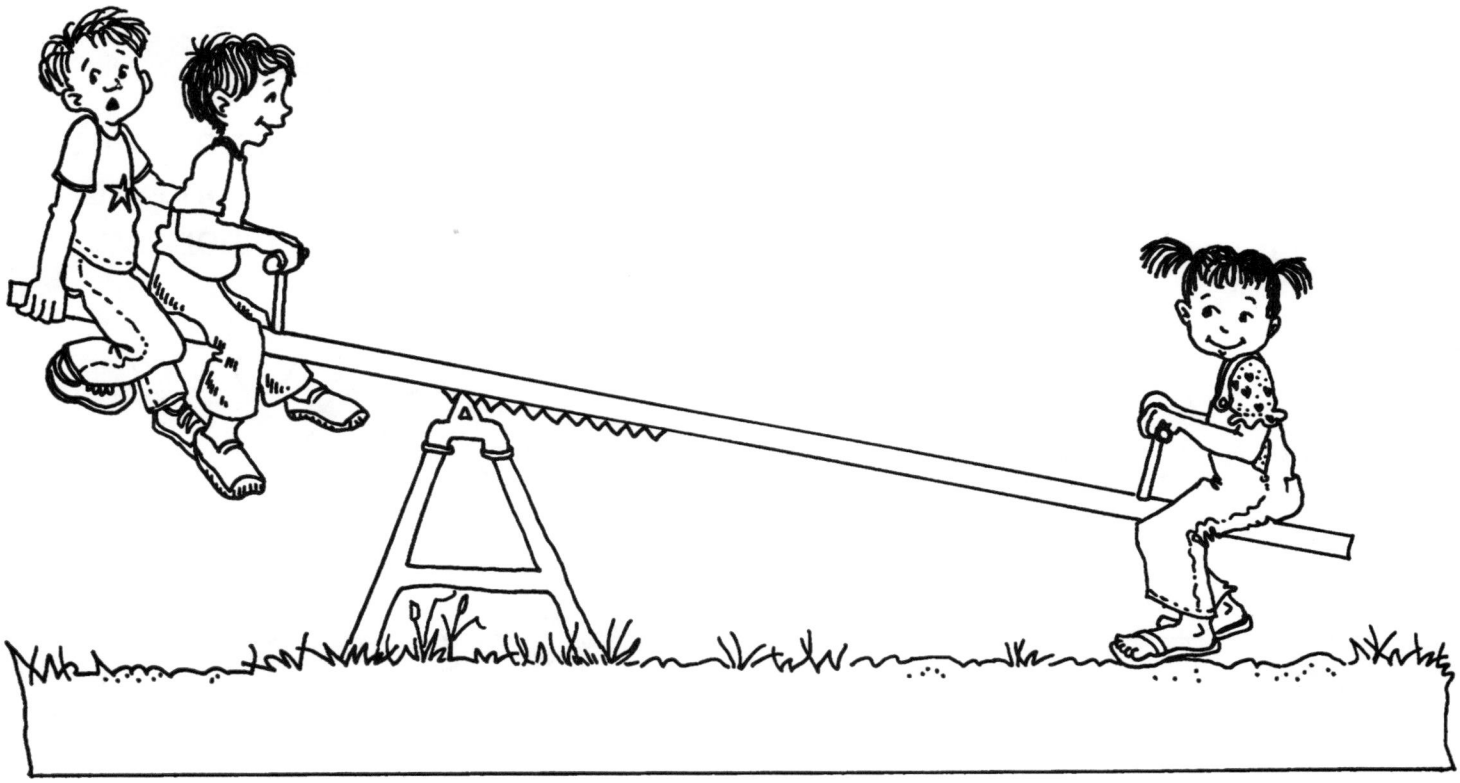

The girl is sitting on the long part of the seesaw.

Because her side of the seesaw is longer and heavier,
she can lift the boys.

You can lift an adult in the same way.

The long part of the seesaw on your side would help you.

Name_____

 Copyright ©2001 by Incentive Publications, Inc., Nashville, TN.

For You to Try

Place a ruler on a small building block, like this:

Pretend it is a seesaw.

Place different objects on one end. Lift them up by pressing with your hand on the other end.

Can you lift things with the ruler?

What kind of simple machine is the ruler when you use it in this way?

Write it.

lever

Name_____

Copyright ©2001 by Incentive Publications, Inc., Nashville, TN.

Which Truck Will Go Faster?

This board is resting on a small block of wood.

If the toy truck is placed at the high end of the slope, it will roll down.

This board is resting against a chair.

If the toy truck is placed at the high end of the slope, it will roll down.

Circle the truck that you think will roll faster.

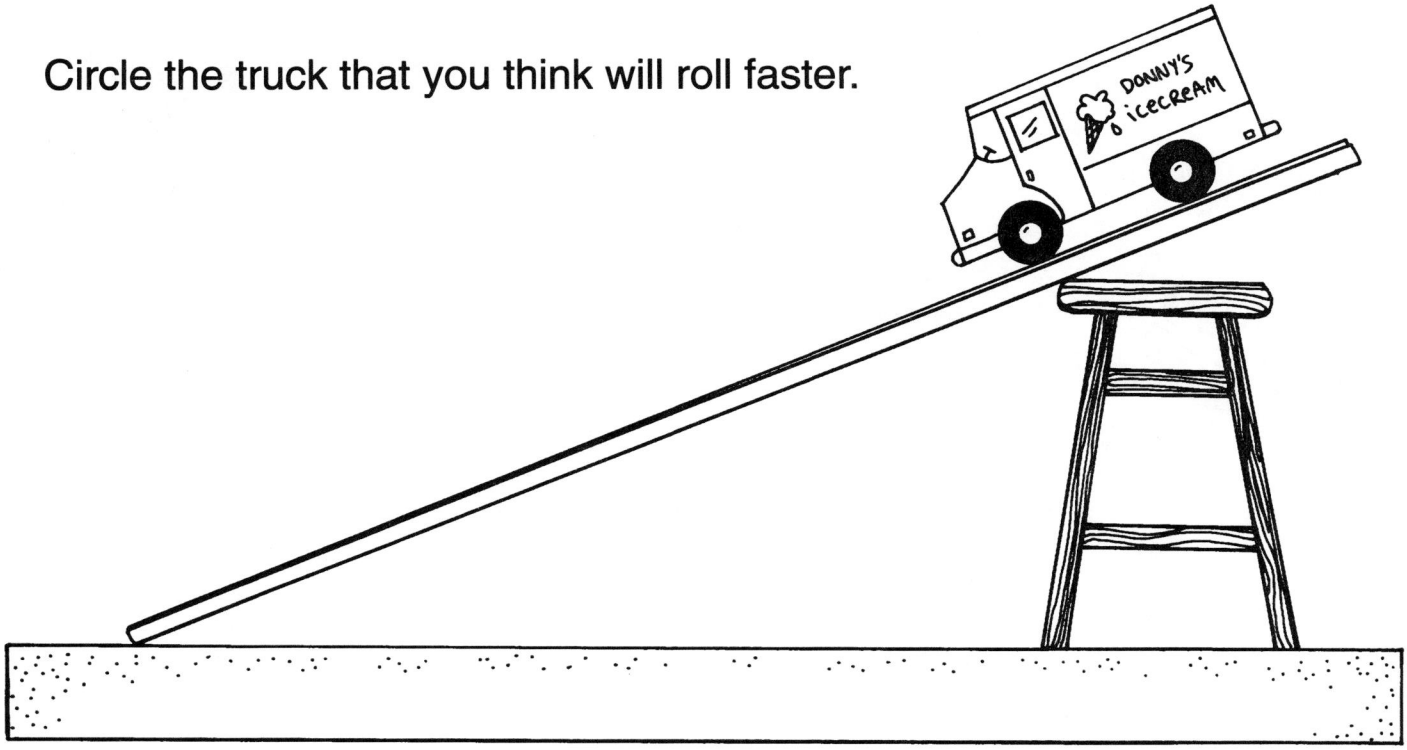

Name_____

 Copyright ©2001 by Incentive Publications, Inc., Nashville, TN.

An Inclined Plane

If you said the second truck will roll faster, you are exactly right!

The board under it is higher, so the slope is steeper.

A board used as a simple machine is called an <u>inclined plane</u>.

An inclined plane makes going up and coming down much easier.

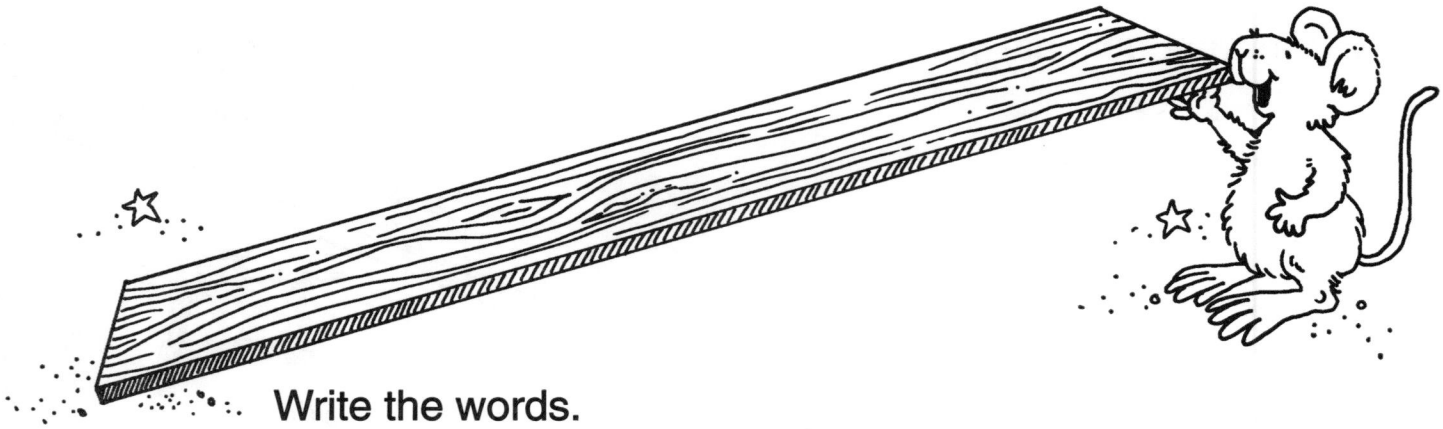

Write the words.

inclined plane

Name_____

 Copyright ©2001 by Incentive Publications, Inc., Nashville, TN.

Take a Big Step

What a big step!

Only a giant could do it easily.

A boy or a girl would not be able to get up on the landing without help.

An inclined plane can help.

A stairway is an inclined plane.

Draw another inclined plane that will make the big step easier.

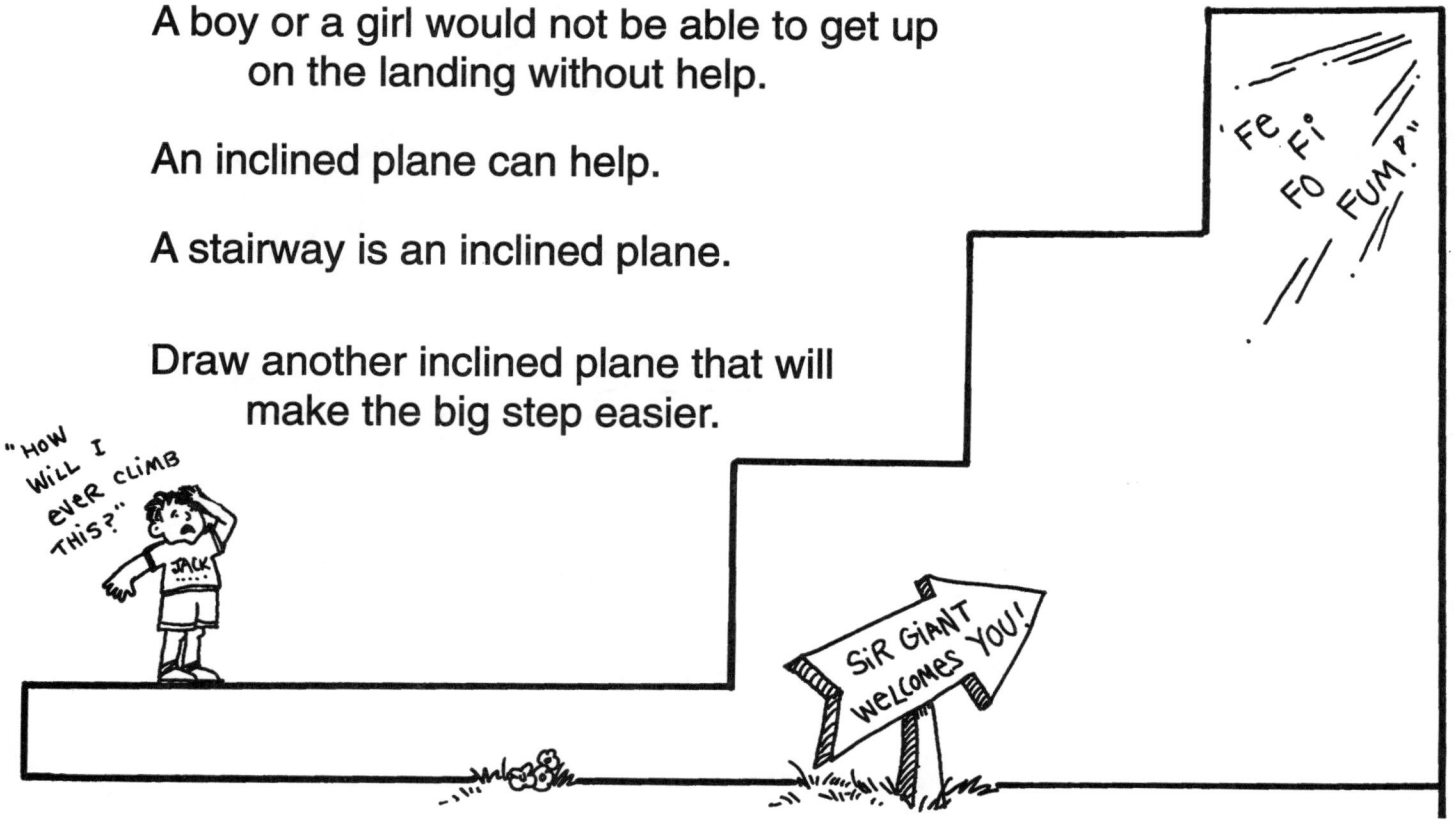

Name_____

Copyright ©2001 by Incentive Publications, Inc., Nashville, TN.

Move the Box

What machine could these children use to help move the box more easily?

Follow the dots to find out.

Name_____

 Copyright ©2001 by Incentive Publications, Inc., Nashville, TN.

Many Machines

There are many different kinds of machines.

Color the machines on this page.

Circle the things that are not machines.

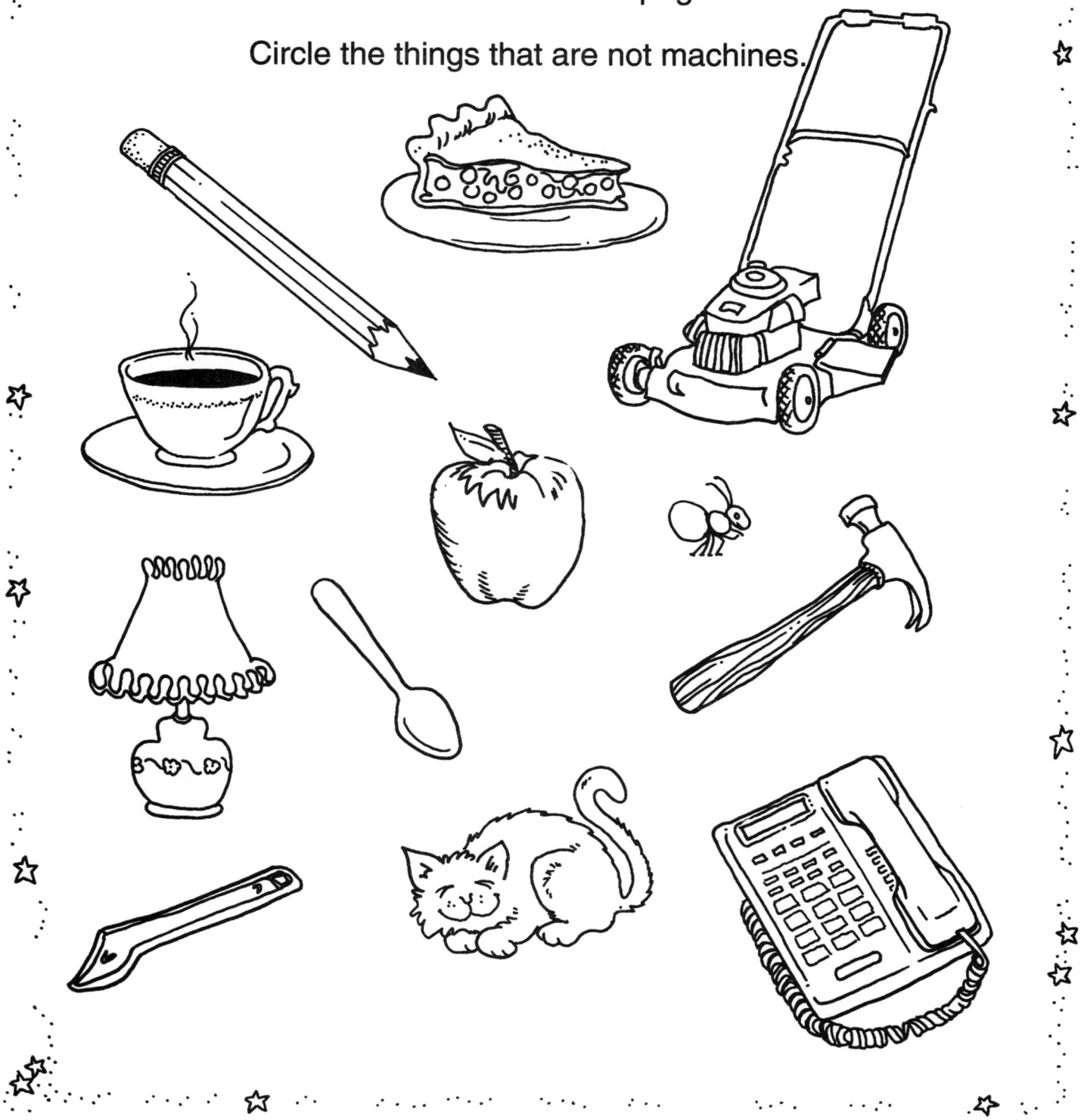

Name_____

 Copyright ©2001 by Incentive Publications, Inc., Nashville, TN.

Machines to Make Work Easier

Cut out the pictures and paste each one in the correct box to show how a machine could make each person's task easier.

 Copyright ©2001 by Incentive Publications, Inc., Nashville, TN.

Thank Goodness for Machines

Look around the room to find a machine that makes life easier.

Draw a picture that shows how you would have to do this machine's work if the machine had never been invented.

Name_____

 Copyright ©2001 by Incentive Publications, Inc., Nashville, TN.

Can You See Electricity?

Electricity is all around us.

It is in the air, on the ground, and in the things we touch.

But we can't see it.

We can only see what it does.

Color the things in the picture that need electricity to work.

Can you think of one more thing that electricity can do?

Name_____

 Copyright ©2001 by Incentive Publications, Inc., Nashville, TN.

How Electricity Helps Us

Electricity gives us light.

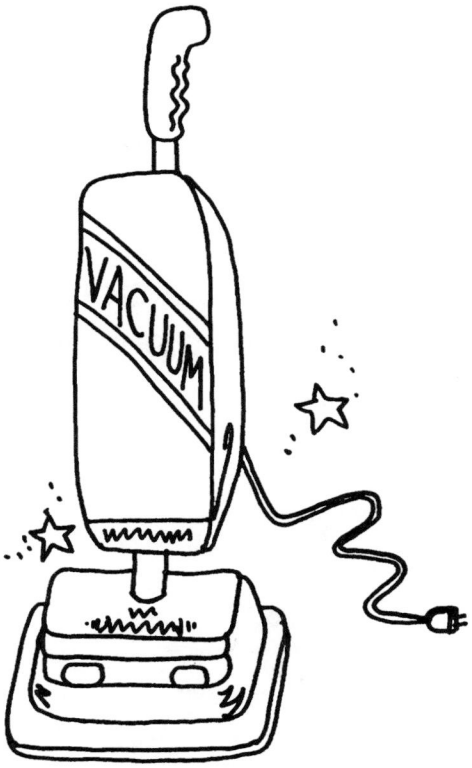

Electricity gives power for tools and machines.

Electricity gives power for TV, telephones, radios, telegraphs, and radar.

Electricity makes things move.

Electricity gives us heat.

Name_____

 Copyright ©2001 by Incentive Publications, Inc., Nashville, TN.

Electrical Power

Do you know which things get power from electricity?

Draw a circle around each thing that gets its power from electricity.

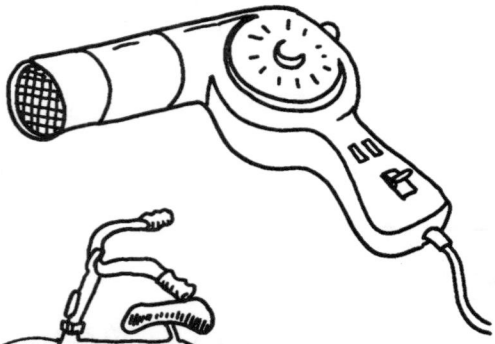

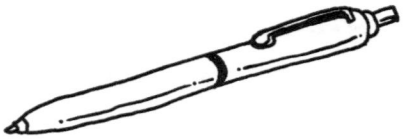

Name_____

 Copyright ©2001 by Incentive Publications, Inc., Nashville, TN.

Magnets

A magnet is a stone or a piece of metal that can pull things toward it.

Magnets can pull or attract or pick up only things that have the metals iron, nickel, or cobalt in them.

Draw a circle around the things that you think a magnet could attract.

Color them.

Name_____

 Copyright ©2001 by Incentive Publications, Inc., Nashville, TN.

This is My World

You have been studying about the world and your place in the world.

Draw a picture of your world.

Be sure to include plants and animals, sky and earth, and some of the other things you have learned in this book.

And most of all, don't forget to draw YOURSELF!

Name_____

 Copyright ©2001 by Incentive Publications, Inc., Nashville, TN.

Appendix

Test Yourself

Make an X on the picture that shows a tool.

Draw a circle around the pet that is a mammal.

Color the animal that was hatched from an egg.

Draw a dotted circle around the picture that shows winter.

Draw a line under the picture of the object that uses electricity.

Draw a dotted line under the picture that shows pigment.

Name_____

 Copyright ©2001 by Incentive Publications, Inc., Nashville, TN.

What Have You Learned?

Draw a circle around the picture that shows an insect.

Make an X on the picture that shows night and day.

Color the picture that shows a magnet.

Draw a line under the picture that shows a lever.

Draw a dotted circle around the picture that shows seeds.

Name_____

Copyright ©2001 by Incentive Publications, Inc., Nashville, TN.

Answer Pages . . . Check Yours!

 Copyright ©2001 by Incentive Publications, Inc., Nashville, TN.

 Copyright ©2001 by Incentive Publications, Inc., Nashville, TN.

Vocabulary for Science

Living things
Non-living things
Plants
Animals
Air
Water
Sunshine
Flowers
Vegetables
Stems
Roots
Leaves
Flowers
Seeds
Cuttings
Bulbs
Experiments
Hatch
Mammal

Farm
Pet
Zoo
Insect
Eat
Egg
Habitat
Human body
Heart
Exercise
Rest
Sleep
Growing
Changing
Skin
Protect
Freckles
Virus
Skeleton

Name_____

 Copyright ©2001 by Incentive Publications, Inc., Nashville, TN.

Vocabulary for Science (cont.)

Bones
Brain
Pulse
Healthy
Care
Yawn
Sneeze
Pores
Diaphragm
Blood
Earth
Sky
Soil
Rock
Land
Night
Day
Light
Summer

Winter
Fall
Spring
Season
Space
Wheels
Moon
Star
Tools
Magnets
Electricity
Float
Dissolve
Lever
Pollution
Litter
Evaporate
Rainbow
Fossil

Name_____

 Copyright ©2001 by Incentive Publications, Inc., Nashville, TN.